Railroad to

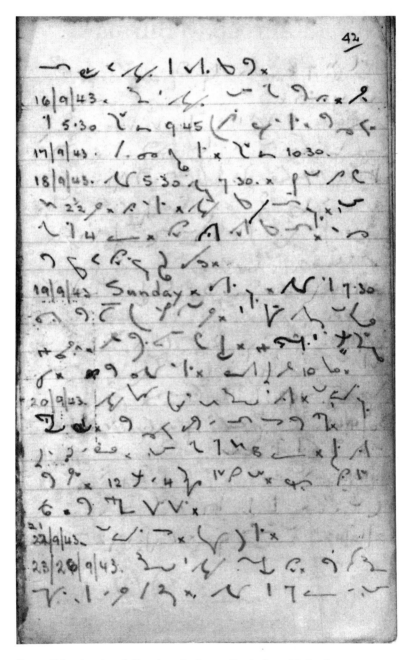

Page of the shorthand diary kept by James Boyle from 23 April to 14 December 1943.

Railroad
to
Burma

James Boyle

ALLEN & UNWIN

*Is life so dear, or peace so sweet, as to be
purchased at the price of chains and slavery?
Forbid it, Almighty God! I know not what
course others may take, but as for me, give
me liberty, or give me death!*

Patrick Henry

© James Boyle 1990.
This book is copyright under the Berne Convention.
No reproduction without permission. All rights reserved.

First published in 1990
Reprinted in this edition 1991
Second impression 1992
Allen & Unwin Pty Ltd
8 Napier Street, North Sydney, NSW 2059 Australia

National Library of Australia
Cataloguing-in-publication entry:

Boyle, James, 1918–
  Railroad to Burma.

  Includes index.
  ISBN 0 04 442151 6.
  ISBN 0 86373 008 7 (pbk)

  1. Boyle, James, 1918– . 2. Burma-Siam Railroad. 3.
  World War, 1939–1945 — Prisoners and prisons, Japanese.
  4. World War, 1939–1945 — Personal narratives,
  Australian. I. Title.

940.547252

Set in 10/11.5 Times by SRM Production Service Sdn. Bhd, Malaysia
Printed by Kim Hup Lee, Singapore

Foreword

J ames Boyle gives an unvarnished soldier's account of the tragic Malayan Campaign and the fall of Singapore. The ill-preparedness, unbalanced forces and defective equipment which sealed the fate of the defenders despite many desperate and heroic areas of resistance are all presented. There follows a first-hand account of the nightmare that was the last days of Singapore and the concentration of defeated troops as prisoners of war in Changi.

The author also records how individuals fared in the early disorganisation and sad disillusionment following the surrender; with praiseworthy measures to restore morale and to defeat the suspension of purpose in captivity. Following the surrender the long battle against semi-starvation, multiple diseases, exhaustion and illtreatment begins.

The total ruthlessness of the Japanese captors surfaced in the Selarang Square incident with the confinement of 15 000 troops in a ground space of some nine hectares, until they were obliged to sign non-escape forms 'under duress'.

The unique feature of the book is a concise day-to-day record of experience with F Force in Thailand. The ghastly story of F Force is an encapsulated drama within the overall horror and heroism of the Burma–Thailand Railway construction. This force consisted of 3662 Australians and 3400 British, already under-nourished and in poor condition.

Railed from Singapore to Ban Pong, Thailand, packed in steel trucks for some four days, they were then destined to carry out night marches over a distance of 300 kilometres for over two weeks with 15 stages, each about 20 kilometres. These marches in monsoon rain and mud, along appalling jungle tracks usually took 12 to 15 hours, and the days were spent in rain-sodden discomfort permitting little rest or medical attention.

They were committed to the remote Thailand extremity of the line about the Three Pagodas Pass at the strained limit of the

Japanese supply line for food, shelter or medicine. Most of the areas of daytime halts on the march were at crude construction camps fouled by the equally ill-used Asian labour force, and had become cesspools of infection, conveying malaria, dysentery and cholera.

The total exhaustion and depletion of the force by sickness and death was countered by frenzied Japanese brutality. By May 1944, 1060 Australians and 2036 British Army troops from F force had perished, constituting 50 per cent of the number. Boyle records at the end of the railway task a death rate of 61 per cent British and 39 per cent Australians.

'Jimmy' Boyle, a wiry man of extraordinary endurance and spirit, not only displayed keen powers of observation and a thirst for enquiry, but was highly competent in concise expression by short-hand. In this way, he recorded the major incidents of his long confinement, but the day-to-day cover of the dreadful march and of the terrible conditions in such camps as Shimo Sonkurei and Kami Sonkurei is quite unique. Only his remarkable tenacity, his command of shorthand, and dogged determination permitted his keen observation to be recorded.

He pays a fine tribute to the inspiring and dedicated services of Major Bruce Hunt, an Australian doctor who battled fearlessly for the sick.

Boyle's return to Singapore via Kamburei was marked by further grave illness with jaundice and dysentery which reduced him to an enfeebled emaciation, close to death. His slow recovery was due to determination and a very tough constitution. His stamina was severely tested later when at the end of a terribly exhausting day, he carried a collapsed workmate, in pouring rain, for four kilometres back to camp.

Following his ultimate return to Australia James Boyle's life once again became very busy and fruitful, marked by an additional sustained contribution to ex-POW welfare. To this he brings both compassionate zeal, and powers of organisation.

I commend *Railroad to Burma* to those who appreciate an account of gallantry and stoic endurance, well told.

Sir Edward Dunlop
A. C., C. M. G., O. B. E., K. C. S. J.
M. S., F. R. C. S., F. R. A. C. S., F. A. C. S.,
D.Sc. Punjabi (Hon.) LL. D. Melb. (Hon.)

Contents

Illustrations

Maps

Preface

16.9.43   Worked on railway. Knocked off very late. Rose at 5.30
arrived home 9.45 after raining nearly all day. Very
miserable.
17.9.43   Much the same as previous day. Arrived home 10.30.
18.9.43   Reveille 5.30 should have been 7.30. Sat in rain for about
two and a half hours. Rained all day. Railway passed our
camp today. Knocked off at 4 o'clock. Line laid right past
camp. All men very pleased that line completed so far as we
are concerned.

S uch were the few details I was able to record in my small
shorthand notebook during the long working hours of a few
days before the sleepers and rails were finally placed in position past
our camp at Kami Sonkurei in Thailand. The morning of the 18th
September had started badly, but it was the one for which all of us
had waited and prayed for nine nightmarish months.

As the first train chugged past our camp I wondered whether its
driver gave a thought to the thousands of men who had given their
lives so that Nippon might build a railroad to Burma. Our boys were
not thinking of the value of the railway to Nippon when some of
them gave a rousing cheer as they heard the whistle of the diesel as
it passed our camp. Most of us, however, simply heaved a silent sigh
of relief that our 'hell on earth' was now nearing an end.

Sixteen hundred men of F Force already lay buried along the line,
and many more were to die later as a result of the diseases and
hardships endured. Nippon's railway from Thailand to Burma was
now almost completed, and we were to take back to civilisation the

remnants of our ill-fated F Force, which suffered more casualties than any other force on either the Burma or Thailand sections of the railway.

None shall know the hardships, the sufferings, the humiliations our men endured. None shall know the thoughts that died with those we left in the burning embers of fires in the bamboo-covered jungle. Only those of us that were returning knew what we saw, endured and somehow survived.

Beneath the rags and the grime of those who limped back to Singapore stood some of the finest men to have worn an Australian uniform. Theirs had not been the role of the fighting soldier, but one of combat against an enemy whose methods would not have been found in the army training manuals of any civilised nation.

Time can dull the memory of most, but a whole lifetime cannot remove the scenes of misery that are painted indelibly upon the minds, or remove the scars of the filthy tropical ulcers, which maim the bodies of those who returned.

No matter what reparations the Japanese may be forced to make, no matter what restitution they may offer to make, no matter what they may say or do, can ever compensate their victims for the cruel treatment received at their hands.

James Boyle

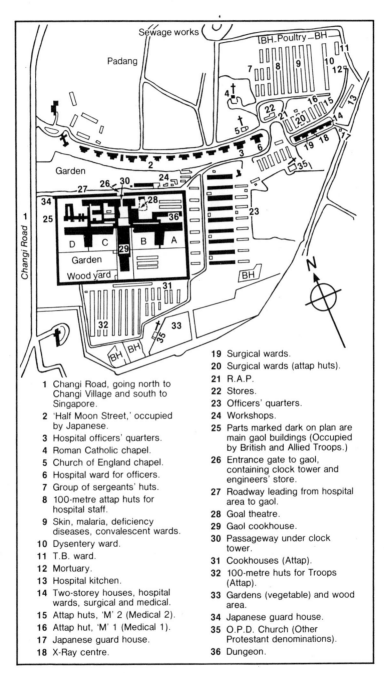

1 Changi Road, going north to Changi Village and south to Singapore.
2 'Half Moon Street,' occupied by Japanese.
3 Hospital officers' quarters.
4 Roman Catholic chapel.
5 Church of England chapel.
6 Hospital ward for officers.
7 Group of sergeants' huts.
8 100-metre attap huts for hospital staff.
9 Skin, malaria, deficiency diseases, convalescent wards.
10 Dysentery ward.
11 T.B. ward.
12 Mortuary.
13 Hospital kitchen.
14 Two-storey houses, hospital wards, surgical and medical.
15 Attap huts, 'M' 2 (Medical 2).
16 Attap hut, 'M' 1 (Medical 1).
17 Japanese guard house.
18 X-Ray centre.
19 Surgical wards.
20 Surgical wards (attap huts).
21 R.A.P.
22 Stores.
23 Officers' quarters.
24 Workshops.
25 Parts marked dark on plan are main gaol buildings (Occupied by British and Allied Troops.)
26 Entrance gate to gaol, containing clock tower and engineers' store.
27 Roadway leading from hospital area to gaol.
28 Goal theatre.
29 Gaol cookhouse.
30 Passageway under clock tower.
31 Cookhouses (Attap).
32 100-metre huts for Troops (Attap).
33 Gardens (vegetable) and wood area.
34 Japanese guard house.
35 O.P.D. Church (Other Protestant denominations).
36 Dungeon.

Changi Gaol area (see chapter 15).

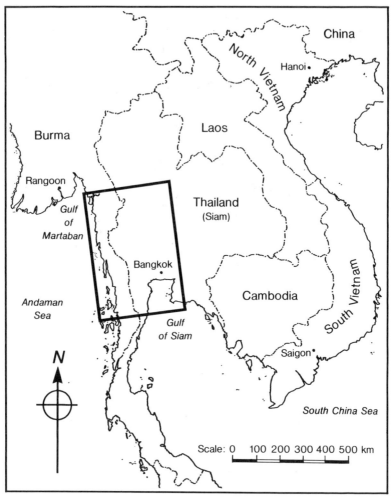

South-east Asia: showing location of the Thai–Burma railway

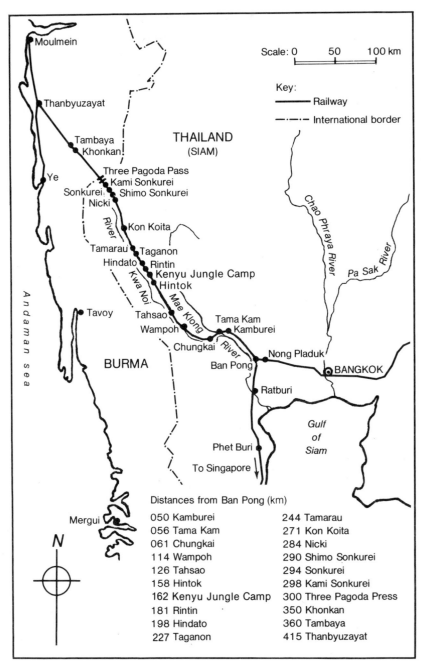

The Thai–Burma railway

Dedicated to
Alf 'Snowy' Macklin

Died Singapore 21 July, 1945

1

The defence of Malaya

When the first contingent of the 8th Division AIF was sent to Singapore during the early months of the year 1941, it was with a feeling that the island they were being sent to defend was an impregnable fortress, the undoubted bastion of our Far Eastern British defences. History books recorded this belief; in fact, the world believed that in the improbable event of hostilities, Singapore could withstand a siege for an unlimited period.

When, however, hostilities broke out with Japan on 8 December 1941, the defences of both Singapore and the mainland of Malaya were in such a deplorable state that it soon became evident that the long-held belief in the security of both regions was a myth.

The combined defence forces of the navy, army and air force were totally inadequate to withstand the potential might of a hostile power in the latter part of 1941. Far Eastern Headquarters was aware of the position, but repeated requests for a complete review of the situation relating to the present antiquated aircraft and equipment and the fast deteriorating state of the coastal defences, aerodromes, etc. invariably met with little response from Whitehall.

By the time Far Eastern Headquarters was able to convince the authorities of the seriousness of the situation it was, unfortunately, too late. An extensive programme of aerodrome construction was embarked upon; it was decided to modernise aerodromes already partly constructed and to commence new aerodromes large enough to handle modern bombers and fighters, in areas chosen by RAF Headquarters to be the most suitable.

Although it should have been quite obvious that the defence of such aerodromes in Malaya would become the responsibility of the army, the RAF failed to consult or seek advice of the army's GOC

The author, age 22, taken at Malacca in Malaya, June 1941.

Malaya, which lack of cooperation met with regrettable consequences immediately hostilities commenced.

The Japanese invading forces first landed at Kota Bahru, where one of the newly constructed aerodromes was situated within 30 km of the coast. Lacking the essential army defence preparations, they provided little resistance to the establishment of a land base from which Japanese aircraft could operate. Similar blunders were made in the construction of aerodromes in other areas, the sites being far too close to the coast and insufficiently manned to successfully defend them against a strong invading force.

It was the policy of the British government at this time to withhold despatch of modern fighter planes and bombers to Singapore, based on the conclusion that they were needed to a far greater extent in other theatres of war. Thus was retarded the already slow progress of the defence of Singapore and Malaya, so vital to peace in the Pacific.

Even in the latter months of 1941, the only planes at the disposal of the RAF in Malaya were Brewster Buffalos and Vildebeest types,

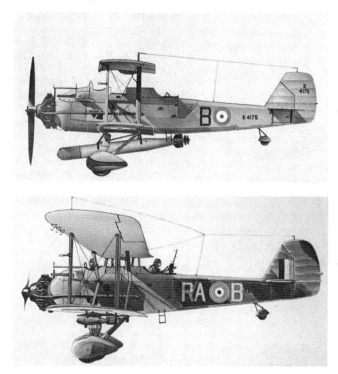

These illustrations of the Vildebeest Mark III used from 1937 to 1942 show the antiquated aircraft which our pilots were expected to use to defend Malaya.

models which were at that time antiquated and completely unfit for combat against the modern aircraft of any potential enemy.

The Japanese discovered this pitiful state of affairs after their very first bombing raid on Singapore island on 8 December 1941, and proceeded thereafter to concentrate their attention on the numerous docks, godowns, and supply dumps, knowing full well that their attacks would meet with little successful resistance from our defending aircraft. These attacks were all the more effective because of the special bomb sight developed by the Japanese, which facilitated extreme accuracy against ground targets, even from very great heights.

Allied pilots flying old-fashioned aircraft could not be expected to ward off bomber attacks escorted by modern fighters of the Zero and Navy O type, planes of far superior manoeuvrability and speed. Our aircraft were outclassed at every turn, even though the pilots of the RAF and RAAF did all in their power to maintain the reputation established by their brothers in the defence of England's shores against the German Luftwaffe. The hopelessness of their task in defending Malaya can be readily appreciated when it is remembered that 90 per cent of our fighter planes were shot down in aerial battles against the overwhelming supremacy of the Japanese.

Air HQ Malaya found, as the war progressed, that it could not spare more than four or five fighter planes to combat the persistent Japanese bombings, which invariably consisted of formations of 27 twin-engined bombers escorted always by their fighter planes. These fighter escort planes were equipped with a 'belly' petrol tank attached to their undercarriages, which greatly increased their range for long-distance raids. The tanks could, if necessary be released at a moment's notice. It is hardly surprising, then, that Allied airmen met with little success during the initial stages of the campaign.

In December–January 1941–42 the Japanese concentrated their attention on the bombing of poorly defended aerodromes and, what is more important, on the bombing of front-line troops who were becoming demoralised by the persistent dive-bombing attacks and the Allies' apparent inability to prevent them. The Japanese land forces naturally took advantage of these attacks to push forward their advantage. Our troops soon became more or less accustomed to such attacks, realising that whenever they took up any new position, its defence would rest entirely on their own shoulders, because of the lack of air support.

Much to the delight of everyone, a small consignment of Hurricane fighters from England arrived at Singapore toward the end of the campaign, and hopes of remedying an almost hopeless situation began to rise.

Upon arrival of these Hurricanes at Singapore naval dockyards, the crates were immediately unloaded, the machines were assembled and were being tested in the air within 48 hours. However, even after the first two or three days it became quite obvious that the number of planes sent would be quite inadequate to make any real difference. Within the first week of combat, 25 of the 51 Hurricanes had been lost.

Shortly afterwards, a further batch of the same planes arrived at Palembang aerodrome in Sumatra, and these were immediately flown over to Singapore to join the squadrons already operating. A third consignment reached Sumatra early in February 1942, but because of the danger of aerial attack whilst in port, the ship upon which the planes were being transported was forced to anchor well out to sea while the planes were assembled.

This action of course necessitated a take-off from the flight deck of the carrier, but according to a flying officer attached to the squadron very few of the pilots had received any training in this difficult undertaking. The task was however successfully accomplished after some rather unorthodox take-offs, which the officer found highly amusing until his own turn came to depart!

When this third batch of Hurricane fighter planes were flown to their base at Palembang, preparations were made for their immediate departure for Singapore island, where they were to join the earlier arrivals. However, word was received from HQ at Singapore that no further newly arrived planes were to be sent across until all machine guns on the planes had been carefully inspected. The previous batch had gone into action with the barrels of their guns still clogged with grease!

The Hurricanes undoubtedly proved their superiority to the Japanese Navy Os during the short time they were in action in Malaya, and had the number of planes been brought up to a more sensible figure prior to the outbreak of hostilities in December 1941, the outcome might have been different. It was a case of too few, too late!

• • •

Prior to the capitulation of Singapore the staff attached to Air HQ together with the few remaining aircraft evacuated Singapore and departed for Java, where they no doubt intended to continue the rather one-sided combat for air superiority.

It seems hardly necessary to pass opinion on the downfall of Singapore. It was quite obvious to anyone who followed the campaign that lack of air support for both the navy and army, and lack also of cooperation between the three services were contributing factors. Modern warfare cannot be fought successfully without the complete collaboration and cooperation of navy, army and air force, and it would appear that the Battle of Malaya, where this cooperation was notably absent, provides a telling illustration of this essential factor.

Eventually, it led to the abandonment of all hope of holding Singapore, our self-styled island fortress of the Far East.

So far as Allied naval strength at Singapore was concerned, it was found impossible to spare more than a few cruisers and destroyers, normally attached to the China Station, for operations in Malayan waters. This despite the fact that, from a strategic point of view, defence would depend to a great extent on our naval power.

Singapore newspapers plastered their front pages with reports of the arrival of HMS *Prince of Wales* and *Repulse* in Pacific waters a few days prior to the outbreak of hostilities on 8 December 1941. The only logical reason for the departure from normal naval convention of strict silence regarding their movements seems to have

---

Singapore
10 February 1942.

To all Unit Commanders:

It is certain that our troops on Singapore island heavily outnumber any Japanese who have crossed the Straits. We must destroy them.

Our whole fighting reputation is at stake and the honour of the British Empire.

The Americans have held out in Bataan Peninsula against far greater odds. The Russians are turning back the picked strength of the Germans. The Chinese, with an almost complete lack of modern equipment, have held the Japanese for four years and a half.

It will be disgraceful if we yield our boasted fortress of Singapore to inferior enemy forces. There must be no thought of sparing the troops or civilian population and no mercy must be shown or any weakness in any shape or form.

Commanders and senior officers must lead their troops and if necessary die with them. There must be no question or thoughts of surrender.

Every unit must fight it out to the end and in close contact with the enemy.

Please see that the above is brought to the notice of all senior officers, and by them, to the troops,

I look to you and your men to fight to the end and prove that the fighting spirit that won our empire still exists to enable us to defend it.

(signed)   A. P. Wavell.
General.
G. in C. South West Pacific.

General Wavell popped into Singapore for a day or two then promptly left! He wrote several letters to cheer up the troops, the first is transcribed above.

been a gigantic bluff planned to convince any potential enemies of the naval power surrounding Singapore!

However, these tactics proved ineffective, as within 48 hours of their departure from the Singapore naval base during the first week of December 1941, HMS *Prince of Wales* and HMS *Repulse* became victims of the Japanese Fleet Air Arm. Both British ships were bombed and sunk in an engagement with torpedo bombers in the Gulf of Siam.

Japanese dive bombers attacked both ships from every angle, making it impossible to elude the dozens of torpedoes launched at close range. The Commander of HMS *Repulse* successfully eluded as many as sixteen torpedoes during the action, but after receiving no fewer than six direct hits was finally compelled to order his crew to 'abandon ship'. A similar fate befell HMS *Prince of Wales*, which went down with flying colours an hour and a half following the sinking of the *Repulse*.

Commanders of both vessels had refused to remain at anchor at the Singapore naval dockyards in the Straits of Johore, where they might have presented a perfect target for the daily Japanese bombing attacks. They knew there to be inadequate air protection for either vessel, so chose to take their chances on the high seas, knowing also that no fighter protection would be afforded them once they left port.

If further proof was needed by London of the disastrous neglect in the pre-war planning for the defence of Singapore, it was soon made perfectly clear by the catastrophic sinking of the *Repulse* and the *Prince of Wales*. In a quotation from the London *Daily Express*, the Singapore *Straits Times* declared on 13 January 1942:

> While this fight goes on, it becomes clearer every day how much Japan owes to the crop of incompetent British windbags . . .
> The time is too short for ordinary methods of truth-telling and publicity to retrieve the situation. But if Gen. Wavell sees fit to take the most drastic measures against slothful officialdom, he will have the thanks of the whole Alliance.

The only other naval action of any consequence in these waters took place in the Sunda Straits when USS *Houston*, a cruiser attached to the American Asiatic Fleet, and HMAS *Perth* found themselves on 28 February 1942 somewhat unexpectedly in the centre of a large Japanese convoy, and succeeded in sinking at least 39 of the enemy craft before they themselves were sunk.

Following the fall of Singapore on 15 February 1942, Allied naval strength was concentrated in Java. Toward the end of the month, there were five cruisers—HMS *Exeter*, USS *Houston*, HMAS *Perth*, HNMS *De Ruyter* and *Java*, three British destroyers HMS *Electra, Encounter* and *Jupiter*, four American destroyers and two Dutch destroyers.

After an engagement with the Japanese in the Java Sea, the *Exeter* and *Encounter*, together with the four American destroyers limped back into the port of Sourabaya on 26 February 1942. However, within 48 hours one of the Dutch destroyers was bombed and sunk in the harbour and the *Exeter* and *Encounter* were also sunk after a further engagement with the enemy. The remaining four cruisers HMAS *Perth*, USS *Houston*, HNMS *De Ruyter* and *Java* sailed from Sourabaya but the two Dutch ships were sunk shortly afterwards.

```
            I M M E D I A T E.




                                      G (I)
                                      Staff Msge. Control
Comdr. 3 Ind. Corps.                  Chief Cipher Officer.
Comdr. Southern Area.
Comdr. A.I.F.
"A"
"Q"
C.A.A.D.
B.R.A.
C.E.
C.S.O.
D.D.S.T.
D.D.M.S.
D.D.O.S.
D.P.M.


          It has been necessary to give up the
struggle but I want the reason explained to all ranks.
The forward troops continue to hold their ground but the
essentials of war have run short.

          In a few days, we shall have neither petrol
nor food.    Many types of ammunition are short, and the
water supply, upon which the vast civil population and
many of the fighting troops are dependent, threatens to
fail.    This situation has been brought about partly by
being driven off our dumps and partly by hostile air and
artillery action.    Without these sinews of war, we cannot
fight on.

          I thank all ranks for their efforts
throughout this campaign.


                              (signed)  A.E.Percival.
                                        Lt. General.
                            General Officer Commanding
                                        Malaya Command

"G"   (Ops).
15th Feb. 1942.
```

Formal advice from G. O. C. Malaya Gen. A. E. Percival to all commands of his decision to capitulate. It was written on 15 February 1942. The author had access to such letters and was responsible for the decoding of all secret messages to his unit.

HMAS *Perth* and USS *Houston* were the sole surviving cruisers and they were ordered to pass through the Sunda Straits and make for Tjilatjap on the south coast, to assist in evacuation of Allied personnel. Just before midnight on 28 February 1942, the two ships ran into a large flotilla of Japanese naval ships and transports.

Both these ships had previously been notified by the Dutch authorities in Java that Sunda Straits was quite clear of enemy shipping. The survivors from both vessels were later picked up by the Japanese on and around the islands, and spent their days as prisoners of war in Malaya, Java, Burma, etc.

Japan did not completely ignore the boasted reports regarding the defences of Malaya, but secretly trained her navy and air force to such a degree of perfection that when hostilities commenced, we were surprised to find just how well-trained and well-equipped her troops really were.

We had been led to believe by the monthly pamphlets and literature supplied to us by Malayan Command prior to hostilities, that the Japanese Air Force was untrained, inefficient, and hardly likely to attempt any air raids at night. It was explained that the Japanese had failed to carry out any night attacks during operations in China, also that they were reported to be inefficient marksmen because of their poor eyesight! Results achieved by their gunners and bombers proved the utter stupidity of the British and Malayan Command intelligence services. The rubbish we were fed was unbelievable.

By contrast to our own lack of knowledge of Japanese competence, it became patently obvious immediately after the first week of the fighting, that the enemy was well acquainted with the disposition of all our land forces, and other invaluable information regarding our defences.

The Japanese displayed remarkable efficiency in their fifth-column activities during the whole campaign. Prior to the outbreak of hostilities, they had military representatives dispersed all over the Malay peninsula and Singapore, ostensibly carrying out duties as rubber planters, photographers, tradesmen, etc. These 'fifth columnists' were, however, secretly gathering detailed information relating to arrival of convoys, distribution and location of our troops through the mainland and Singapore, and studying the topography of every region, information which was invaluable when their forces later invaded Malaya.

Back in Japan, they not only studied thoroughly in the classroom during the day, but also did their homework at night, so that in December 1941 the picture of the Singapore and Malaya situations in Tokyo HQ was probably far more accurate than that possessed by Whitehall.

The Japanese also employed local natives to act as guides during their advance down the peninsula, and on several occasions Tamils or Malays were sent forward as scouts to gain information regarding our positions. The difficulty of the front-line troops was compounded by the fact that the population of Malaya is of Malay, Indian and Chinese extraction—the latter in particular were difficult for inexperienced western eyes to distinguish from the Japanese.

Naturally, the forward areas contained natives both in uniform and civilian dress and any number of these might have been in the employ of the Japanese. Any suspicious actions on the part of a native led to investigation, though some were shot immediately as spies.

Some of the very simple methods adopted by the fifth columnists, and the means by which they were readily recognisable to the enemy, consisted of the wearing of coloured arm-bands, dresses or sarongs; washing arranged in a particular pattern on a clothes-line; and dry palm leaves painted white, and formed into an arrow pointing in the direction of our troops in the vicinity.

At Kuala Lumpur in the state of Selangor, a few days before its capture by the Japanese, the suspicion of the authorities was aroused when they learned that some of the locals had been seen leaving a well-known Japanese bicycle shop; on inspection it was found the handle bars contained maps giving the location of our troops all over Malaya. The bicycles were apparently intended for the use of the Japanese upon their arrival at Kuala Lumpur. Fortunately the scheme was frustrated.

Lieut. General Sir Lewis Heath, Commander of 3rd Indian Corps cited a further instance of fifth column activities in the engrossing lecture he gave at Changi prisoner-of-war camp shortly after the fall of Singapore. He said that information regarding the activities of a certain smuggler had been made known before the outbreak of hostilities, but because of lack of sufficient evidence the authorities could not make an arrest. When Japanese transports later approached the northern coastline of Malaya at Kota Bahru, their small landing craft were, by the smuggler's guidance, able to effect a successful landing at night in otherwise difficult waters.

The efficiency of the fifth column organisation in Malaya undoubtedly assisted the Japanese invasion and played an important role during the campaign, similar to that played by the agents of Germany when her troops invaded France and other European countries in 1939–40.

The Malayan campaign consisted of a series of withdrawals down the northern sections of the peninsula. It proved impossible for the British to hold their positions for any length of time, due mainly to the infiltration methods adopted by the enemy and the latter's efficient training in jungle warfare. However, on several occasions

4th Motor Transport tug-of-war team, Malacca, June 1941. Back row: Jack Lambell, Roy Ritchie, Norm Lane, Jack Hodge. Front: Joe May, 'Snowy' Gowers, 'Tiny' Jenner, Bill Cook.

our land forces temporarily stopped the advance of the enemy, and according to the men themselves could have maintained their positions for a considerable length of time, had they not been given orders to withdraw!

At Muar, on the west coast, in the southern state of Johore, about 150 km north of Singapore, men of the 8th Australian Division held their positions longer than any others in the whole campaign. The Japanese Commander, General Yamashita later admitted that the savage fighting at Muar held up their plans for four days. In spite of the brevity of this somewhat belated victory, our front-line troops temporarily regained confidence in their ability to stop the monotonous regularity of the enemy advance, and the constant infiltration behind our lines.

Infiltration had an extremely demoralising effect, especially at night, when rifle fire from our rear indicated the presence of enemy troops, signalling the fact that they had somehow penetrated our lines. It was often impossible to see more than a hundred metres because of the dense undergrowth, which prevented the use to advantage of the larger machine guns. The 2/4th West Australian Machine Gun Battalion, which did such a magnificent job in the defence of Singapore island in February 1942, was more or less sacrificed in being sent to Malaya. Vickers machine guns were totally unsuited for conditions there, although it must be admitted that on the few occasions when the opportunity presented itself the men of this battalion used their machine guns to deadly advantage.

The Japanese landing barges presented an admirable target for these well trained machine gunners when they attempted a crossing of the Straits of Johore at a point close to the causeway, and another on the northern tip of the island. The Japanese later discovered that this particular battalion was responsible for causing so many of their casualties. Soon after capitulation Japanese guards went to the battalion's unit headquarters and took away several officers and men, stating that they were required as drivers. It later transpired that they had been taken away to face a firing squad. The report was brought back by the battalion sergeant major, who faced the firing squad but succeeded in escaping by pretending to be dead, and waiting until the Japanese had left the area.

Much has been said and written about the treatment of prisoners taken by the Japanese at the height of battle, and it is beyond doubt that the Japanese committed some terrible atrocities during the campaign that coloured forever the perceptions of those who witnessed them.

The atrocities they performed during the war and in the years of occupation afterwards, proved them to be in no manner, shape or form, anything but a pack of uncivilized barbarians.

The fall of Singapore on the afternoon of 15 February 1942 did not come as a great shock to most of us; it required no great intelligence to appreciate the hopeless position of our forces during the last days. However, when final orders arrived from Headquarters to lay down our arms a fit of depression overtook us, followed by anger — at having become victims of one of the war's greatest blunders.

It is no use attempting to compare the evacuation of Greece or Crete to that of Singapore. No opportunities for evacuation existed, except for the few who 'shot through' before capitulation, or immediately afterwards.

Orders were given by Headquarters during the last few days that any of our men attempting to escape by means of small craft were to be intercepted or fired upon from the various small islands scattered around the south coast of Singapore. Very few attempted to get away, and most of those who did decide to take the risk of clearing the islands were ultimately intercepted by Japanese destroyers patrolling the waters for such escapees, or were machine-gunned by aircraft on patrol for the same reason.

No doubt the authorities were justified in adopting the attitude they did towards escapees, whose actions were tantamount to desertion. Nevertheless, I am firmly convinced that some attempt would have been made to clear troops from Singapore had our governments then had any conception of what allied prisoners would suffer, and of the vast number of casualties that would result from the three and a half year term as guests of Nippon.

• • •

The last days of Singapore were a nightmare, the Japanese dive-bombers continuously harassing front-line troops while the larger bombers concentrated on targets in the city proper. The area occupied by allied troops comprised a very small proportion of Singapore island during the last few days.

Friday February 13 — Black Friday — will be remembered by everyone in that small remaining area, soldiers, civilians, men, women and children alike, as one of the most disastrous days of the whole campaign. I have heard it said by British soldiers who took part in fighting in France during the German invasion, and who were also unfortunate enough to be sent out to Malaya, that the last days of Singapore were comparable to the evacuation at Dunkirk. The Japanese met little resistance in their bombing raids and it could always be taken for granted that any planes in the sky were those of the enemy. 'Air raid red' therefore continued for 24 hours of every day.

The actual order to cease fire was given late in the afternoon of Sunday 15 February 1942, after General Percival and General Yamashita had completed negotiations at the Ford Motor Works at Bukit Timah.

The air which that same afternoon had echoed to the blast of shell fire, ack-ack, and the rat-tat of machine-guns now became strangely silent, and slowly we came to realise that our efforts to defend the island had been in vain. The grim faces of the men proved that beyond a doubt.

In spite of the fact that the men had not slept for nights past, their reaction to the changed conditions, the absence of the clamour and racket to which they had become accustomed, made it difficult for anyone to rest. The following morning found men in small groups discussing the pros and cons of the changed situation and what conditions might be as prisoners of war. No restrictions were as yet placed on our movements, so my cobber Jack 'Long Tack' Thompson and I decided to take the opportunity to explore the streets of Singapore and inspect some of the damage.

Every street, lane and *padang* was packed to capacity with motor vehicles, armoured cars, and tanks and other army trucks camouflaged by light and dark green paints. The spoils of a victorious enemy! Hundreds of the vehicles had, however, been either burned or damaged to such an extent as to render further use impossible.

The stench of burnt human flesh polluted the air and the bodies of air-raid victims were still being recovered from the entangled masses that had once been buildings. Trucks of the Indian Army Services Corps were still smouldering after an air raid the previous day, when they were caught parked together in a small area close to the docks. Some of the drivers and men had been in the trucks when they were bombed—their bodies were cremated when the trucks caught fire.

Intermittently Japanese staff cars would pass, bearing the simple camouflage of one or two green palm fronds tied lengthways on the hood of the vehicle. Very few Japanese soldiers were to be seen in the city itself, orders having apparently been issued preventing them from so doing. However, their guards and sentries had been posted at vital points and selected buildings which they intended to occupy.

As the day wore on, though, the 'little men of the flaming circle' began to filter into the city borne by push-bikes, motor-cycles, trucks and cars, and those less fortunate, on foot. We found their discipline, which we learned later to be instilled more by fear of their officers than anything else, to be quite good, and the soldiers seemed only to be interested in strolling around the streets on a sightseeing tour.

The Japanese are said to have been surprised when they learned the actual number of prisoners on Singapore island. It amounted to something like 90 000 troops, including Australian, British and Indian.

British troops at capitulation   33 981
AIF troops at capitulation   14 991
Total   48 972

Arrangements for our transfer to a concentration area were therefore not completed during the first 24 hours, and we were left to fend for ourselves until such time as instructions were received from Japanese Headquarters.

On the afternoon of Tuesday February 17 we heard that food supplies at the 10th Australian General Hospital and 2nd Convalescent Depot (then occupying the Cathay building) were almost depleted, so several members of our unit decided to make use of our time by endeavouring to remedy the situation. Fortunately, we knew of several good food dumps and as motor transport was still

"2/1 AUST. HOSPITAL SHIP, 'MANUNDA,' A.I.F."   Painting by John Allcot

Manunda *Hospital Ship card signed by the returning POW nurses. It contains
the signatures of all the surviving nurses of the 8th Division AIF. They were:
Iole Harper, A. B. Jeffrey, Eileen Short, Viv Bullwinkel, Nestor James,
J. Tweddell, S. Muir, J. Greer, V. I. McElnea, V. Clancy, C. Oxley,
C. J. Ashton, J. Gunther, M. Syer, C. M. Delforce, J. E. Simons, Val Smith,
J. Doyle, P. Blake, E. M. Hannah, W. E. F. Oram, B. Woodbridge, Jessie
Blanch, F. E. Trotter.*

available we chose what we deemed to be the best of the supplies—
tinned milk, fruit, pineapple juice, tinned meat and vegetables,
etc.—and set out for the hospital at the Cathay building.

Our progress through the city was not interrupted by the Japanese,
so we decided to risk a couple more trips. The hospital staff and
patients were extremely grateful.

This hospital, which occupied the ultra-modern Cathay picture-
theatre, was hit by a shell a few days before capitulation. The shell
penetrated the extremely light roof structure of the theatre, and
burst on the balcony. The blast caused a number of deaths to
walking patients who were resting on the balcony, and severely
affected others who were already shell-shocked.

The lounge of the theatre was filled to capacity with men lying
about on the floor—very few beds or stretchers being available. It
was pitiful to witness the plight of the shell-shocked cases, whose
limbs were continually twitching and whose faces showed the tension
and strain of the past weeks. Sleep, if it could be found, was their
only respite.

Our nursing sisters had been evacuated from Singapore in two
groups just prior to capitulation. The second group of 65 left
Singapore on the *Vyner Brooke* on February 12, and 12 of these lost
their lives after their ship was bombed and sunk before reaching
Java. Fifty-three nurses made it to the shore, but the Japanese
massacred 21 of them shortly afterwards. Sister Vivian Bullwinkel
was the sole survivor, and along with nurses from other areas was
taken prisoner by the Japanese. Thirty-two nurses became POWs
but only 23 survived the ordeal of their three and a half years of
captivity.

Men from different units scattered around the island of Singapore
were able to enjoy a complete rest during the few days following
capitulation, whilst awaiting movement orders from the Japanese.

On Wednesday 18 February 1942 instructions were received that
all personnel were to move under their own steam to Changi area
on the east coast, a march of some 24 km from the heart of
Singapore.

2

Changi

W hen the order came for the removal to Changi, our own unit, the 4th Motor Transport Company, was given permission to retain several of our 3-tonne Marmon Harrington Trucks. We were thus able to transport most of our personal gear, and a vast amount of tinned foodstuffs. In the interval between our arrival at Changi and the Japanese commencing to supply us with rations this tinned food was invaluable, as most of the units had no supplies whatsoever.

For the men who were forced to march, it was one which they have no doubt remembered when longer marches of their training days are forgotten. Everyone was worn out by the strain of the past few weeks, and all were burdened with whatever clothing and food they had been able to accumulate. No one knew how long we would be prisoners of war. Just as well we did not!

In the extreme heat of the day, the march proved beyond the stamina of hundreds, with the result that units which had moved off from Singapore as a body during the morning were strung out for miles before completion of the march. Foot-sore and weary, men straggled into Changi camp all night interested in nothing other than something to eat and an opportunity to rest.

Changi was probably the best area that could have been chosen to house the vast number of British and Australian prisoners of war, as the camp itself represented the extremely large peace-time barracks of the British garrison. The climate too was claimed to be the best on the island (that is if the climate of any part of Singapore can be said to be good!).

The barrack buildings were solid two- or three-storey concrete structures, fitted out with showers, latrines and other facilities.

An artist's impression of a typical Changi mess parade.

Several of the buildings had received direct hits from bombs and shells, and temporary repairs were made in order to make them habitable.

Hundreds of the men arrived at Changi possessing only the clothes they were wearing, black from oil smoke and filthy from the mangrove swamps they had trudged through during the battle. A change of clothes had not been possible during the last week and water was still scarce.

Our first issue of fresh water was on the Thursday morning (February 19), and consisted of half a pint per man. This was taken from a nearby well, and had to last us until a further supply was brought by truck from the city proper. The main water supply line was, of course, out of action due to bombings.

Feeling as we did, any sort of water clean or otherwise was welcome, so when Long Tack and our other close mate, Alf 'Snowy' Macklin and I discovered a large cement drain with water half a metre deep, it answered our requirements admirably, in spite of the fact that it carried slimy salty swamp water on the rising tide from the Straits of Johore. We had the satisfaction of feeling cooler — albeit dirtier and smellier — than when we started!

We very soon discovered that lack of water would be a very serious problem to the whole camp. The men were thrown on their own resources to obtain supplies.

The old maxim that 'necessity is the mother of invention' was never truer than in the case of the POWs in Changi and other camps throughout the Far East over the ensuing three and a half years, when regular systems broke down, or materials and apparatus became unavailable or worn out.

Several men from my own unit under the supervision of driver Arthur Whatley, from Donald in Victoria, devised a system by which they could pump water from a nearby underground water-course up to the buildings in which we were then billeted, and to our cookhouses, etc. They set to work to scrounge suitable pipes and hand pumps for the purpose, dug wells, set up their apparatus, and within 24 hours were drawing a seemingly endless supply of icy cold spring water.

How the gear was obtained, and where it came from, the Lord only knows, but pumps for several other wells were also operating within a very short space of time. However, as was the case with water from most sources over the next few years, supplies from the new well had first to be boiled before being fit to drink.

We were always careful to take whatever precautions were necessary to maintain standards of hygiene, and boiling of any water was one of the essentials. Regrettably, it seems that the subject of hygiene receives scant attention during the elementary training of private soldiers. The matter is left to those specialising for certain sections or units. We prisoners of war came to realise just how essential the strictest hygiene was to the maintenance of the health of our troops.

Within a very short time following our arrival at Changi camp, it became obvious that we were in for a lean time so far as rations were concerned. We knew there to be huge food dumps all over the island but the Japanese had apparently decided to utilise these to feed their own troops, who were at that time preparing to occupy Java, New Guinea, and other islands of the South Pacific, on their way to Australia.

Lack of food supplies was our most serious problem as POWs from the first till the last day. Very few of us had experienced the pangs of real hunger in our own countries, but that indefinable something that exists down in the pit of the stomach when food is scarce caused many an unhappy day and night to all of us in various camps throughout Malaya, Thailand, Burma, and so on.

A really hungry man, I mean one who has not eaten a worthwhile meal in months, will do practically anything, and eat practically anything, to appease that appetite. Snails, frogs, dogs, cats, and even rats were cooked up and eaten by some of our men in order to relieve that empty feeling.

As soon as supplies did commence to arrive at our main camp ration store at Changi, we learned to our dismay that it consisted of rice and very little else. Naturally, this sudden change came as a blow to many, who found it difficult to adapt to the new diet and allowed their health and weight to suffer as a result. One of the strangest consequences of the change in our diet was the refusal of our bowels to function normally. Believe it or not, one chap in our unit went for 31 days without passing a motion!

Almost everyone immediately began to lose weight. The rations issue was extremely light and although rice is admittedly filling, it is composed mainly of water and is not a great body builder. Rice remained our staple diet for three and a half years. Three times a day, seven days a week, fifty-two weeks a year.

Our cooks soon began to experiment with ways to make the rice more palatable. They discovered that by grinding the rice grains it was possible to make rice bread and small 'doovers' (cakes or rissoles). We gradually adapted to eating the local native food which was issued from time to time by our hosts. Stinking dried fish and blachan (a name given to fish that is buried in the sand for a long period, then retrieved) were often delivered to the camp, but were at first invariably dumped into the refuse bins. However in time we

327

AUSTRALIAN MILITARY FORCES

Records Office,
Victoria L of C Area,
252 Swanston Street, C.1

25th. June.   1942

Dear Madam,

      With reference to my recent letter informing you of the absence of news concerning your

brother, Number VX.45598. Corporal James BOYLE,

    4th Reserve Motor Transport Company A.I.F.

      I am directed by the Minister for the Army to advise you that he must now be posted as Missing and to again convey to you his sincere sympathy.

      Your natural anxiety at the non receipt of further particulars is appreciated and you are assured that everything possible is being done by the Department and through the International Red Cross to obtain further news, on receipt of which you will be immediately notified by telegram.

      Yours faithfully,

Lieut. Col.,
Officer-in-Charge Records.

Mrs. E.I. Pascoe
5 Love Street,
HARTWELL.

T.G. 42.   COMMONWEALTH OF AUSTRALIA—POSTMASTER-GENERAL'S DEPARTMENT.   Office Date Stamp

Funds may be Quickly, Safely and Economically Transferred by MONEY ORDER TELEGRAM.

TELEGRAM

This Telegram has been received subject to the Post and Telegraph Act and Regulations. The time received at this office is shown at the end of the message.

The date stamp indicates the date of reception and lodgment also, unless an earlier date is shown after the time of lodgment.

Sch. C.3873—7/1942.

Office of Origin. 5. Melbourne 40/1   No. of Words. 2-5p   Time of Lodgment.

Postal Acknowledgment Delivery Personal

Mrs E I Pascoe
5 Love St
Hartwell

J Boyle prisoner of war I have to inform you that VX45598 Boyle J previously reported missing is now reported prisoner of war
    Minister for the Army

3-15p tl

Two of the messages conveying news of James Boyle during the first few years as POW. They were both sent to his sister, Mrs Edith Pascoe.

found ways to eliminate the smell slightly, having learned by this stage never to discard anything that might be classed as food, no matter how repellant it might seem to Australian tastes. Items such as dried fish soon became acceptable to the majority of us, although some chaps found it impossible to stomach the stuff without later dire effects.

White flour was on issue for a short while, and the Field Bakery Unit went into action, constructed an improvised bakehouse and began to produce quite a good loaf, considering their makeshift facilities and lack of proper ingredients. Yeast, for instance, was made from the milk of coconuts.

For some reason or other, salt became difficult for the Japanese to supply in any quantity at Changi, and it was found necessary for various units to send a party of men to the beach each day with 44-gallon drums and other suitable containers to collect salt water.

* * *

How long we were doomed to remain guests of the little men of the flaming circle was something of an unsolvable problem in 1942, though of course plenty ventured a guess, some expressing the opinion that we might be released before Anzac Day.

Time lay heavily on our hands during the first few months, so it was decided that in order to relieve the monotony it would be a good plan to commence training classes and instruction in a varied range of subjects. It was not surprising that among the thousands of prisoners at Changi were numbered some prominent businessmen from Australia and England, as well as barristers, technicians, accountants, tradesmen, engineers, lawyers, etc. who were only too eager to impart their knowledge to anyone interested in sparing a few hours with them each day.

Classes were generally conducted during the day, with the evenings being given over to lectures or discussions which always attracted large numbers of chaps interested in extending their knowledge. Without a doubt, there would have been many who returned home in 1945 equipped with a knowledge they could not possibly have acquired in peace time. Whether they would admit that the knowledge they acquired was worth the sacrifice of three and a half years as a POW is, of course, another matter.

As was to be expected in such circumstances, wirelesses were not permitted by the Japanese. However laws were made to be broken and this proved to be no exception so far as Changi camp was concerned, and many radios were assembled from the parts which had been brought out from Singapore. Naturally, a certain risk was attached to their use, but it was justified because the news proved always of great benefit to the morale of the men who were thus able to keep in touch with the progress of the war.

Sometimes it was found necessary to withhold reports of important actions in certain theatres of war, because of the risk of irresponsible individuals discussing news gleaned from the BBC news, which often reported actions before they were published by the Japanese in the local press.

During the first few months of captivity, sources of information were not always as reliable as they might have been. All sorts of rumours circulated (always guaranteed as to their authenticity of course, the news having emanated from a pal in another unit, who knew another chap who was in some way connected with someone who heard it on the radio). Our life as prisoners hinged on the ever-present existence of furphies (rumours) and the possibility that they might be authentic, hoping all the time of course for news of our imminent release. It would be impossible to record the number of times Germany capitulated, for some optimists amongst us, between 1942 and 1945!

In May 1944 there was a very strong rumour that the Nazis had capitulated toward the end of the previous month. This report appeared to have some substance when, during the next week or two, the Japanese newspaper *Syonan Shimbun* published details of the long-awaited establishment of a second front in Europe. Reading between the lines of this edifying journal, the landing appeared to have met with certain initial successes.

We felt sure that we were at that time well on the way to final victory against the Axis powers, especially when the attitude of the Japanese administration appeared to change slightly to one of cooperation with our own Headquarters and surprising acceptance of suggestions for improvement in conditions. Previously, any requests met with a stone-wall refusal to consider them.

• • •

During the earlier stages of our captivity in 1942 the sudden hardships we all had to face were made easier for some who were fortunately equipped with sufficient British Malay currency to tide them over for a period. Such men were able to convert their cash into foodstuffs available at times from the local traders.

At the time of capitulation, it was not known whether the Japanese would recognise our British currency, but fortunately they decided that for the time being at any rate our money would be negotiable. No arrangements were made for the opening of canteens during the first few months, but this did not prevent men from obtaining food and cigarettes, of which there was naturally a shortage with a correspondingly constant demand. Many took the risk of 'shooting through' the wire at night to contact local natives for supplies. Prices were exorbitant, especially to the eventual buyers, a loaf of bread being $1.50, and tins of bully beef and milk $3 to $4

Singapore River pre 1941.

when a loaf of bread at home would have cost the equivalent of 3 or 4 cents. The 'black market' profiteers and racketeers were in their element, but to give them their due a great element of risk was attached to the procuring of any such items outside the surrounding camp wire.

Despite the danger, black market activities continued at intervals during the whole three and a half years, even though the Japanese warned us frequently that anybody caught outside the wire would be severely dealt with. Some were caught, and paid the resulting penalty of being shot.

As the months wore on a few battle casualties, previously reported as 'missing' or 'killed in action', began to drift into Changi. Some of these chaps had been wounded in action, and loyal Chinese had taken them into their own homes, sheltered and cared for them until they had recovered sufficiently to make their own way to a POW camp. One chap waltzed into Changi bearing the marks of 29 bayonet wounds! His life was spared by nature, in the form of maggots which ate the rotting flesh, and prevented deadly gangrene from setting in.

Medical officers worked day and night caring for the sick, and although ex-POWs are apt to complain about our officers—often with some justification—I have yet to hear a bad word spoken of any medical officer of the 8th Division.

Our medical officers were undoubtedly responsible for maintaining not only the health of our troops, but also the morale, and set a wonderful example for all to follow. Men had unquestioning faith and confidence in the ability of any doctor — physician or surgeon — and considering the lack of adequate medical supplies during the whole three and a half years, their achievements were nothing short of miraculous.

Such men as Major Kevin Fagan of H Force, Lt. Col. E. E. Dunlop (Dunlop Force), and Major Bruce Hunt of F Force, all skilled surgeons on the Burma railway, were beyond any shadow of doubt worthy of the admiration and high esteem in which they were held by all ranks. The hospitals in which they had to work were hospitals in name only, and in some cases were more like pigsties.

During the month of March 1942, the Japanese first began to draw upon the fit men at Changi for working parties to be sent to smaller camps in Singapore to act as labour gangs at the docks and godowns, loading their ships and performing other odd jobs. Other parties consisting of carpenters, tailors, drivers, etc. were also called for, and many who followed these particular trades in civilian life were only too eager to do something to relieve the monotony of Changi camp.

One party numbering about 600 was sent to a small island called Blakit Mahang, which is situated just off the coast of Singapore. Contrary to all conventions, this party was engaged in handling ammunition and loading it on to Japanese ships, working from early morning till late at night under extremely difficult conditions. Sometimes they were forced to remain on the job continuously for several days, without any sleep and with very little food. The Blakit Mahang working party was not a permanent one, and was at irregular intervals relieved by a fresh gang from Changi.

On Easter Saturday of 1942 (April 3), a party of about 2000 Australian and British troops, myself included, was moved out of Changi camp. We were led to believe that the job would occupy about two to three weeks. We were therefore instructed to take a minimum of clothing and other requirements, and told that we would have to march the 30-odd kilometres to our new camp carrying our gear. None of us felt at all like marching far — we were at that time fairly weak, and not yet accustomed to our new diet from which we did not appear to be deriving much benefit.

As we progressed toward the city, the Singaporeans brought out their baskets loaded with bread and small cakes, tinned pineapple and so on, and offered these to the boys at reasonable prices. After the confinement and the spartan diet of the previous few months, the trip seemed more like a picnic than anything else.

The long march however began to take its toll as we approached the outskirts of Singapore proper and small groups, tired and limping, gradually began to fall back behind the main column. Late in the afternoon the Japanese, realising that at our present pace we would not reach our destination by nightfall, decided to pick up the stragglers by truck. We all eventually finished the last few kilometres in this fashion, for which we were extremely grateful.

Our new camp was known as Adam Park. It was close to the Bukit Timah Road, about 2 km from the Singapore Golf Course.

3

Adam Park

A dam Park at first sight gave little cause for celebration. The two-storey brick buildings in which we were to be housed were shell-torn, roofless in parts and littered with debris. We were compelled to clean up the mess in order to find sleeping space. The place absolutely stank. Every room was damp and a perfect harbour for 'mossies', from whose dive-bombing attacks we suffered all night.

Up to the time of our arrival at Adam Park, we had received no indication as to what our work was to be. Late on the night of our arrival, we learned from camp HQ that half the men who had arrived that day would be required to march out to the Singapore Golf Course next morning to build a road.

You can imagine the reception such a report received from the men. Some of our blokes had believed until they became POWs that 'Manual Labour' was a Spaniard! Very few of us had ever handled a pick or shovel, except perhaps occasionally in the garden at home, and did not relish the idea of spending our time as road builders for Hirohito. By next morning the outlook did not appear any brighter, but we decided that it was time to start getting used to the idea.

On our first day at the golf course very little work was done, as the Japanese in charge seemed to have as much idea of road construction as we did, and in any case we were not keen to be of assistance. The day was a fiasco, there seemed to have been absolutely no prior planning or preparation.

On the second day some of us were permitted to stay in camp, and we soon set about making our new quarters as comfortable and as clean as possible in the circumstances. The houses had been occu-

27

pied in peace time by government administration staff. The area had
been in the centre of the fighting toward the end, and some of the
houses were quite uninhabitable, but the majority were soon in
quite good shape after a bit of repair work. Some of the furniture
still remained in the houses, but most items of value had been
looted after the occupants fled Singapore.

The gardens and coolie quarters in the vicinity of the houses
contained dozens of rudely constructed graves. On the cement floor
near the doorway of the native quarters at the rear of our house was
the imprint in dry blood of a soldier's body; legs and arms out-
stretched where he had apparently fallen after being shot. Another
soldier lay in a shallow cement drain nearby with a small covering of
earth over him. After his identity had been established, we buried
him in the back garden of our house.

Our first task was to wash and clean out our building and make
repairs to the tiled roofs while others in our party dug bore-hole
latrines, the septic tank system having been put out of commission.
By the time the working party returned from the golf links at about
6 pm we had the place looking quite presentable, although there
was still plenty more to be done.

The Japanese next day decreed that every man, with the exception
of those who were sick, was to be sent out on the road. From that
day onward the pressure was on, and we had very few days off and
plenty of hard work to keep us occupied.

We were marched out in the early morning with our pick, shovel
and 'chunkle' on our shoulders to toil the day in hot sun or
torrential rain. There had been a general belief that it was impossible
for a white man to work under the tropical sun — we soon con-
founded that theory, and I for one and plenty more began to thrive
on the hard work. We learned to wield a pick and shovel as well as
any expert road worker back home, and on a plain rice and no
trimmings diet too!

Under the eagle eye of the Japanese we began to establish the
outline of a road around the border of the golf course, but from the
outset we could see, even with our inexperienced eyes, that it was
going to be a complete failure. The Japanese in charge knew little if
anything about road construction, and the only interest we ever
showed was when one of them yelled out *Yesame*, which was a
signal for all to 'down tools' and rest for a few minutes in the shade
of a nearby rubber tree.

Days were generally hot and long, and in the extreme heat the
sweat poured from our bodies, saturating the few clothes we wore.
Soon we began to change colour, and the lads in some cases were
almost as dark as the Malays themselves.

As was to be expected, the continued sweating brought about severe attacks of tinea and dermatitis. Some of the cases were quite serious, especially as treatment for such diseases had to be rationed. Scrotal dermatitis or 'Bukit Timahs' as the boys called it was forever a source of worry, both to the sufferers and the medical officers. One can now laugh remembering the poor chaps waddling down the road each morning — with legs splayed and arrayed only in g-strings and wooden clogs — to attend sick parade and have their Bukit Timahs painted!

A long time later in our captivity, a better treatment with a palm-oil base was concocted, but at Adam Park the only relief was by dabbing the affected area of the anatomy with Condy's crystals. Patients were often issued with small dosages in order to treat themselves until the next sick parade. Soya bean sauce, it must be added, is definitely not to be used for the same purpose, as one chap discovered to his horror when he reached for his bottle in the dark one night and mistakenly took down the wrong one from the shelf!

The Japanese apparently concluded that the road job would not prove to be a huge success if they allowed their front-line troops to continue supervision of the road gangs, and replaced them with a batch of army engineers.

Rather than carry our tools back to camp each evening, it had been our practice as we walked along the narrow embankment across the McRitchie reservoir, to dump our spades, shovels, picks, or chunkles in the lake. The Lord only knows how many tools there are at the bottom of the reservoir, but the new gang of Japanese checked our tools each night and soon put a stop to this practice.

In addition to road construction around the Singapore Golf Course, the Japanese proposed building a wooden bridge across the McRitchie reservoir, leading to a large Japanese shrine on the hill overlooking the reservoir and the golf course. Their ideas might have met with approval of the Japanese people, but we were the poor unfortunates they expected to build them!

The pile-driving on the bridge soon put a damper on the would-be carpenters amongst our volunteer workers who reckoned on the job being an easier one than belonging to a road gang. It is not easy to drive piles when you are standing up to your chest in water, especially when someone is standing over you with a solid piece of bamboo cracking it over your skull when you stop. Try it sometime!

The wooden bridge when completed was about 140 m long, and wide enough for two cars, but no nails were used anywhere. It looked alright when it was finished; in fact the Chinese in the carpenters' sheds (not on the bridge) commented that it would burn very well!

It was on the bridge job that the men began to report ill-treatment at the hands of the Japanese. Many men returned to camp in the evening complaining about the treatment they had received, but in spite of repeated protests to the Japanese Command, the bashings continued.

One young chap was pile-driving on the bridge when a Japanese engineer suddenly attacked him with a pick handle, finally knocking him off the bridge into the water. Apart from blows to his head and shoulders, the Australian's arm was so badly damaged that it never really recovered. Another chap who was working on the bridge saw what had happened and jumped into the water and dragged him out. Neither knew one another.

Some 30 years later, Alec Smith from Geelong was on a tour of Singapore with a group of ex-prisoners and their wives. He was telling his friends the tale of his bashing with a pick handle when another ex-POW, Ned Monte from Albury, announced that it was he who had dragged Alec out of the water and saved his life! They became close friends from that day on.

On another occasion, the Japanese engineer in charge of our party began grunting and growling in an effort to make us work harder. Three or four of our chaps foolishly enough began to mimic him. He suddenly grabbed an axe, attacked one of our chaps, and split his head open. Ern Rider survived the attack, but was to die later on the Burma railway after a severe dose of beri-beri.

On another occasion I remember seeing five or six 'Pommies' lined up on the side of the road and receive one of the worst bashings I ever witnessed. A Japanese sergeant discovered that certain concrete reinforcement wire had not been bent to his satisfaction. The sergeant lined them up, stood them to attention, and commenced to bash them about the head and shoulders with a heavy stick, cutting their faces and causing severe bruising. The Pommies did not flinch once, and stood up for more whenever they were knocked down. The Japanese did not stop until he was tired.

In the early stages of working at Adam Park quite a few of our party, including some from the 2/4th Machine Gun Battalion from Western Australia and Graham Campbell for one from our own unit, could not restrain themselves from retaliating when being bashed, and gave the Nips a hiding in return!

Unfortunately, their treatment after we returned to camp in the evening usually took away the pleasure they had had in retaliating for a crack over the skull earlier in the day. Invariably, we were lined up and the culprit was picked out and taken down to the Japanese guard house for punishment.

Most of us had the utmost contempt for these uncivilized barbarians, who seemed to glory in the authority which their new position had given them. In spite of the numerous bashings we received from the Japanese engineers and guards at Adam Park, and the repeated orders by our officers not to fraternise with them, some of our blokes perversely persisted in trying to talk with them during 'smokos'!

While we were working on the road and the shrine and bridge, the Japanese paid us in the new Japanese currency at the rate of 10 cents per day for privates, and an extra 5 cents for NCOs. Pay day became one to look forward to, even though it was often about ten days late. Of course, we could not buy very much with local prices as they were at the makeshift canteen. A few bananas, a coconut, a few biscuits or cakes perhaps, expended our funds very quickly.

There were of course those few who were wealthier than others but most of them earned their money the hard way, at the risk of being caught outside the wire after selling petrol or other saleable commodities to the Chinese. Not far from our camp was the remains of a large petrol dump which had been burned out during the last few days of the battle. A few chaps discovered that some of the drums had remained intact, or partly filled. At $4 a gallon, this was quite a profitable hobby to take up a few spare hours in the evening.

One of the most amusing tales ever to come out of Singapore concerned 'Old Bill' Cummins and his steam-rollers. Old Bill was a member of my unit and a cook in B Section, but at Adam Park he was appointed OC steam-rollers, and given a Japanese arm-band to say so! He was granted a sort of roving commission which entitled him to enter or leave the camp at any hour of the day, merely showing his arm-band to the Japanese guards, without any questions being asked.

Old Bill's roving took him far into the night, when he would leave the camp through the barbed wire (minus his arm-band) and dispose of the day's drawings of petrol from the Japanese storeman on the road job. The idea started when he explained that he would require petrol to start the steam-rollers each morning, and from then on each man appointed to drive a steam-roller on the road would draw his ration before commencing the day's work! Invariably Bill brought his ration back to camp at the end of the day in a 2-gallon drum in a pack on his back. He reeked of petrol, but he was never discovered by the guards.

Old Bill Cummins was a real character, and tales regarding his nocturnal exploits are still told today. One related to a trip outside the wire one evening from which he did not return until long after 'lights out' had been sounded. Naturally, he had been out to sell his precious petrol. Old Bill crept into his room, and endeavored to

4th Motor Transport Company Dvr W. P. 'Bill' Cummins

undress quietly without waking his cobbers. However, his mate Dave Cupples from Woodside in Gippsland was awake and awaiting Bill's return to hear the news Bill always obtained on the outside.

Dave enquired: 'Did you get any news Bill?' Bill was unfortunately afflicted with a severe speech impediment, so he answered: 'It t-t-took t-t-two hours t-t-to t-t-tell m-m-me, it'd t-t-take me all b-b-bloody n-n-night t-t-to t-t-tell you!'

On another occasion, we were working on a back road near the golf course where Old Bill and his steam-roller were also employed. One afternoon he was stricken with a bout of malaria and sent back to camp with the men who had brought out our lunch rations. Naturally, his precious petrol was still stowed safely in the tool box at the bottom of the roller, until a Japanese came along the following morning to start it.

The full tin of petrol having sat in the sun all of the previous afternoon, and for several hours that morning, it was no surprise when the can blew up when the Japanese tried to start the engine. Bill's only response when told of the loss of his petrol was: 'But what about me bloody tin?' There was more petrol where that lot had come from, but a petrol tin was irreplaceable!

A Japanese shrine on the steep hill overlooking the McRitchie reservoir was an after-thought on the part of the Japanese, but it meant a tremendous amount of tiring work for our men. The first task was to clear thick scrub to make way for steps leading up to the shrine.

On the first day, our gang was ordered to clear a strip of jungle about 6 m wide above the water's edge and about 180 m long, and level it off so that the road to be constructed later would be right at the water's edge. We had just commenced to dig out the embankment when it started to pour, and with it came the coldest wind I ever experienced in Singapore. It rained and blew all day, and the water poured down into the cutting we had just started so that soon we were working in sticky mud up to our shins.

Whether the intention of the Japanese was to make the job last as long as they possibly could, or whether they declined to use the modern equipment which was readily available on the island, I do not know, but on the road and shrine they made use of the most primitive methods imaginable. Can you imagine two grown men, sun-tanned and nearly naked, carrying a small basket shaped like a large saucer with a handle on either side, and containing not more than four or five shovels full of earth? Sometimes they had to be carried 100 m or so, so one can readily understand why it took us from April until December to complete the road, bridge and shrine, where between 2 and 3 thousand men were employed daily.

• • •

The incessant work soon became monotonous, each day being much the same as the one before. With the exception of card games and reading there was little we could do in the evenings, until it was decided to form a concert party. Amateur actors and musicians were called for, and within a week we had quite a versatile group of between 30 and 40 artists.

I enlisted my aid as a banjo-mandolinist, and joined the band each evening for practice. The show was capably managed by George Bransen of the 2/4th MG Batt. The orchestra consisting of about fifteen instruments was conducted by Bert Ford of the 8th Div. Sigs, who had been a member of the Melbourne Symphony Orchestra before enlisting.

Some of the instruments were wholly manufactured in our camp, mainly from 3-ply and some of the lighter timber from the house furniture. For instance, chair arm-rests made ideal 'necks' for guitars and banjos. Strings became a problem for a while, until we found that steel signal wire served the purpose admirably. Later on, we made a machine by which we could bind thin coil wire onto D8 signal wire for the heavier D and G Strings of the mandolins and so on.

A new show would be produced each two weeks and would run for two or three nights. They became so popular that some of the chaps would take their evening meal with them in order to obtain a good seat.

The Tivoli Theatre was an open-air affair, and accommodation quite good really. The stage was situated in front of two adjoining cement garages at the bottom of a relatively steep slope, thus affording a perfect view of proceedings besides providing excellent sound effect.

Several popular tunes were used as a base to tell the story of our blissful happiness as prisoners of Nippon. One was sung to the tune of 'In eleven more months and ten more days we'll be out of this caliboose':

> We landed here in Singapore, from cares and troubles free,
> We danced around the cabarets in joyful revelry.
> But now we're POWs, with nothing to delight us,
> And all we've got to show so far, is scrotal dermatitis.

Chorus — In eleven more months, etc

> On eggetty puffs and new laid eggs, and pork & tins of peas,
> For prisoners, gawd strike me pink, we're living a life of ease
> The racketeers are living high, on caviar and pork,
> They'll be so fat when they get home,
> They won't be able to walk.

Chorus — In eleven more months, etc.

> So cheer up lads it won't be long, before we get back home,
> Through Queensland, Vic. and New South Wales,
> We'll soon be free to roam,
> With steak and eggs and onions too, and good sorts there to cheer,
> And oh what a mess we're going to make of a gallon or two of beer.

Chorus — In eleven more months, etc.

• • •

Unlike our fellow prisoners of war in Italy and Germany, we were unable to correspond with our people at home or to receive parcels through Red Cross, and it was beyond our comprehension why the Japanese would not allow these services to be put into operation. It was obvious they were finding difficulty in feeding us, as our diet consisted of about 90 per cent plain rice.

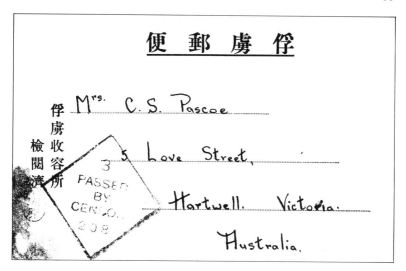

便　郵　虜　俘

俘虜檢閱濟收容所

Mrs. C. S. Pascoe

3 5 Love Street,

Hartwell. Victoria.

Australia.

PASSED BY CENSOR 208

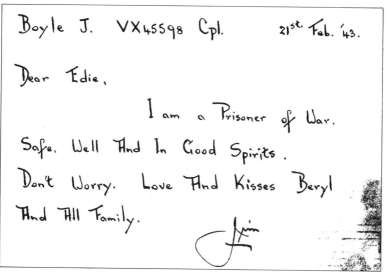

Boyle J. VX45598 Cpl.   21st. Feb. '43.

Dear Edie,

I am a Prisoner of War.
Safe. Well And In Good Spirits.
Don't Worry. Love And Kisses Beryl
And All Family.

Card sent by James Boyle to his sister. This was the second time he was allowed to write home, his first was sent on 2 July 1942.

Toward the end of July 1942 almost everyone at Adam Park was beginning to suffer in some form or other from vitamin deficiency diseases. In September, however, we learned that a shipload of British Red Cross supplies had arrived, and we anxiously awaited the never-to-be-forgotten pleasure of tasting some of our own food

Formal Dinner Officers' Mess
Adam Park POW Camp Malaya.

Potato Crisps, Vegetable Soup
Roast Beef, Yorkshire Pudding
Baked Marrow, Roast Potatoes
French Beans, Green Peas, Steamed Cucumber
Rice Cakes
Gulu Malacca Sauce Iced Coffee
Swiss Roll Savouries, Herrings on Toast
Frozen Water Melon
Iced Pineapple Fingers

An illustration of the disparity between the meals of many officers and other rank POWs. One of the chefs in the Officers' cookhouse was a member of our unit and he made a copy of the menu available to me during our stay at Adam Park Camp in 1942.

once again. After several months we had become accustomed to eating our plain rice breakfast in the darkness before sun-up, spitting out the weevils which it invariably contained, but the inclusion of a drop of condensed milk or a spoonful of sugar or jam gave the meal renewed interest.

Each night would see the workers hurrying back to camp across the cleared rubber plantations and gullies so as to be amongst the first in the mess line, especially if they were in line for a 'back-up' of stew. Eager eyes would be glued on the orderlies, awaiting the call for 'Righto, back-ups starting with L' — or at whatever letter of the alphabet the stew had run out the previous evening.

Naturally the surplus tucker had to be dealt with in this manner, or the 'scavengers' would have been in first for every meal, irrespective of the display they made of themselves. Everyone of us was hungry, and the ration for each had to be the same for all — at least so far as the Other Ranks were concerned.

Great competition sprung up amongst the various unit cook-houses, and if a cook could not produce a meal 'fit for a king' he was booted out to earn his keep with a pick and shovel, and the men appointed an amateur who had done his cooking in the kitchen back home on a Sunday afternoon!

Some of these chaps produced meals our regular army cooks had never heard of and when the cooks began experimenting on the uses to which the new Red Cross rations could be put, the afternoon's topic of conversation on the road would hinge on the contents of the evening's 'doover' or the thickness of the stew. Only too well had we come to know the biting pangs of hunger, and the desperation men can feel at such a time, the misery and helplessness of our position, knowing that we were compelled to rely on our hosts for our very survival.

Despite careful rationing the Red Cross supplies did not last forever and we were soon back to our mainstay — our old friend rice. It was not nice, but at least it kept us alive. One chap in our unit who couldn't force himself to stomach the stuff became another statistic a few short months after our arrival at Changi.

Never at any stage during the three and a half years, did we have more good food than we could eat. We were more or less starved for the whole time, but the Japanese wanted to show to the outside world that they were quite capable of feeding their POWs.

The second and last time I saw Red Cross parcels was on 28 February 1944, the second anniversary of the sinking of HMAS *Perth* and USS *Houston* in the Sunda Straits.

Night-time often turned our thoughts to those at home, from whom we had not heard since the fall of Singapore. When we discovered that the Japanese did not intend to allow the Red Cross service to be put into operation we realised with grave concern that it was possible our relatives and friends at home might not even have been notified of our safety.

In July 1942, however, we were informed that we would be permitted to send a short message by letter card, and were overjoyed at being accorded this somewhat belated privilege. We learned later, much to our disappointment, that despatch of the cards was delayed and they did not begin to filter through to Australia and England until late 1943, by which time thousands who had earlier notified relatives of their safety and good health had died as a result of ill-treatment and poor conditions in the jungles of Thailand and Burma.

It should have been an easy matter to initiate a monthly Red Cross letter-card exchange, but the Japanese remained adamant, and for most of us it was only on three occasions over three and a half years that we were permitted to send short cards home.

Before the fall of Singapore we had always looked forward to mail from home, and its arrival kept us in good spirits. The sudden stoppage was a cruel blow, imposing a great mental strain on some and affecting the morale of the troops as a whole. Our thoughts were our only link with those at home, knowing that they too would be thinking of us — and wondering.

Whilst we were camped at Adam Park, several attempts were made by small parties to escape from the island in an endeavour to make their way to India. Their efforts were frustrated soon after commencement by natives on the peninsula who betrayed their presence to the Japanese.

The 'official' escape party, consisting of Colonel Dillon of the British army and a chosen few, made their escape from Singapore shortly before capitulation, crossed Sumatra, which was at that time occupied by Japanese forces, and were headed for India in a small boat. A Japanese craft stopped to investigate just when success seemed to be within their grasp, and they were eventually sent back to Singapore. Colonel Dillon was later sent to Thailand on F Force, where he was in charge of the British troops at Sonkurai, a few miles from our own camp.

Whenever any of the escapees were captured, they were generally thrown into the civilian gaol at Outram Road, Singapore, and submitted, whether sick or well, to the severest ill-treatment imaginable — solitary confinement on plain rice and water. Some of the chaps, amongst whom was Gordon Rumble of Merlynston, Victoria, who was sent there from Borneo, were confined for twelve months and longer and their condition upon discharge was such that it seems a miracle they survived. Although our conditions and treatment on the Thailand–Burma railroad were bad, I really believe that Outram Road must have been worse, if not the worst of all the places in the East to which POWs were sent.

A large percentage of the chaps at Outram Road goal did not see outside the walls again, and some of those who did, were not strong enough to combat later illnesses resulting from their confinement. However, some did eventually recover, which only makes one wonder at the powers of endurance of the human body.

In his book *Toward the Setting Sun* James Bradley, who was an officer with the Royal Engineers, describes the conditions in Outram Road gaol during his term there in 1943. James Bradley was one of the English officers who escaped from Sonkurai Camp in Thailand. After being in the jungle for six weeks they were betrayed by the Burmese and turned over to the Japanese, tried and sent back to Outram Road gaol in Singapore, where they were kept from October 30 until December 21, 1943.

The Chinese, who had shown true loyalty during the whole campaign, continued to be our friends while we were prisoners of war. At times they took the risk of a bashing from the Japanese guards, yet they would quietly hand cigarettes, cakes, and fruit to our boys on working parties in Singapore whenever they were able, or whisper a word or two of news.

All of the men of the 8th Division have the utmost admiration for the Chinese population of Singapore and Malaya, who proved to be true friends in all our difficult times. No one could alter their easy-going, placid nature, no matter how they were treated. Like ourselves, the Chinese seemed to have confidence that final victory would one day be ours, putting an end to the ill-treatment and hardships that the Japanese occupation of Singapore and Malaya had brought them.

Soon after our arrival at Changi in February 1942 some of our chaps were instructed to report to a certain point on the beach close to the camp, and upon arrival discovered that they were required to bury a number of Chinese men, women and children who had been slaughtered by the Japanese during the 'blitz'. They had been shot with their hands tied behind their backs. Some of the very young children had not been shot, but had apparently been left lying on the sand for several days and had eventually died of exposure.

The Japanese authorities maintained that the Chinese, who had lived in a 'kampong' nearby, had a large supply of military rations to which they were not entitled and believed them to have aided the British forces in the fighting on Singapore island.

Soon after our arrival at Adam Park a Chinese vendor was tied up to a large concrete pillar outside the Japanese guard house because he insisted that one of the guards should pay the price at which he was offering the cakes on his stall. He was bashed with a bayonet, and remained tied up all afternoon and until the next morning. Whenever the guards felt inclined they would come out of the guard house and urinate on him, spit at him, or butt their cigarettes on his head.

The Japanese placed the severed heads of Chinese people on poles in prominent positions in the streets of Singapore — as a deterrent to any Chinese contemplating activity against the Imperial Japanese Army.

The Chinese were forbidden to enter our camp but showed little regard for the order, sneaking through the wire in the very early morning, or in the evenings, when they knew that the men would be in camp. We depended on our friends to provide us with small items of food to supplement our meagre rations, and from them we could purchase fruit, eggs, small cakes (eggety-puffs and curry-puffs), and on occasions tinned food.

One morning, soon after Reveille one Chinese 'mumma' was wandering casually through our house from room to room crying out 'eggety-puffs', 'eggety-puffs', as though she had been doing this same thing each morning of her life. She walked to the bathroom where the boys were showering, popped her head around the door, and enquired whether they wanted any 'eggety-puffs'. Her face did not register any surprise at the sights she had just witnessed, but I did not see her visit our bathroom again!

For their friendship to the men of the 8th Division AIF, the Chinese of Singapore and Malaya will always be remembered. Shortly after the return of the 8th Division, a fund was set up to sponsor nurses from Singapore and Malaya to further their studies in Australia.

4

Selarang Square incident

In November 1942 it was decided to transfer the party at Adam Park to a nearby camp called Sime Road, previously occupied by Royal Air Force personnel, and which actually constituted Far Eastern HQ in peace time. This camp consisted mainly of *attap* huts but the area had been neglected since the fall of Singapore, and was covered in tall *lalling* grass.

The transfer of personnel, bedding, gear and essential cooking utensils, occupied a few days, but the highlight of the move took place when it was time to shift the 'arsenal'. The various nocturnal expeditions between the two camps required a lot of preparation and planning in order to elude the guards who were patrolling the area. Scouts were posted at vantage points along the track, lying flat in the long *lalling* grass. At intervals a head would pop up, there would be a whistle indicating the unwelcome presence of a Japanese guard, and operations would cease until it was 'all clear'.

In this manner, we managed to shift a surprising quantity of ammunition and small arms to Sime Road camp, and of course no time was lost in once again burying these supplies, which would have proved of inestimable value had circumstances provided us with an opportunity of using them once again. However, no such luck was ours while we were at Sime Road, and we were forced to leave the majority of the small arms when we returned to Changi camp at the end of December 1942.

The most noteworthy occurrence of the two months stay at Sime Road was the selection of a party for Japan. They were given a medical examination and equipped with Service dress (our own supplies taken from stores in Singapore) to combat the complete change of climate.

According to my diary, I felt at the time that the treatment of those transferred to Japan would be better than what we had experienced in Singapore. We expected that in Japan itself, perhaps the International Red Cross might take a hand.

We spent our first Christmas at Sime Road, and I think that Christmas Day and Boxing Day 1942 were the most pleasant I spent as a POW, if any day of that period could be described as a pleasant one. We endeavored to enter into the spirit of the occasion (much to the displeasure of camp HQ) and attempted to have as pleasant a time as possible in the circumstances, and I think that to a large extent, we succeeded.

Preparations were made to buy supplementary rations through the Chinese canteen, and the purchase of dates, flour, sugar, fruit, sweet potatoes, etc. helped to make our Christmas dinner the best I ate during the whole three and a half years.

The Japanese graciously presented us with a packet of cigarettes together with a special issue of fresh fish, which were very acceptable. We had also held over a few biscuits and one tin of bully beef per man from the Red Cross rations which had arrived in September, and which were by then considered to be a luxury, in spite of the rude remarks made about this type of army ration in the past.

A few days later we received instructions that we would be returned to the main Singapore POW camp at Changi. We arrived back at Changi on 27 December 1942 and found things to be much the same as when we left, though everyone had settled down and camp organisation and administration showed a noticeable difference, especially in the matter of discipline.

The arrival of our party at Changi coincided with the Japanese evening check parade (*tenko*) and we all thought that we had come across a regimental parade when we saw the troops lined up on the Selarang Square in their Sunday best, wearing shirts, hats and boots, with sergeant majors and officers strutting around like peacocks making sure that none of their men had gone home without leave! We discovered this parade was held morning and evening for a check on numbers by the Japanese. Our officers used to compete to see who could sport the best uniform from their comparatively extensive wardrobes. The state of preservation of some of their uniforms was amazing!

We ourselves had just returned from a working party, not a training camp, and parades (except for work) each morning were few and far between, so the Changi *tenkos* were a bit 'on the nose' to us for a while.

In our absence at Adam Park, most of the high ranking officers at Changi had been dispatched to Japan or other parts of the Far East, and Colonel F. G. Galleghan D. S. O., ED had been appointed Commander of the Australian forces on Singapore. 'Black Jack', as he was popularly known, had proved himself on many occasions to be worthy of the respect shown him by all ranks, and did not fail to carry out his duty as their leader, always doing his utmost to obtain better treatment for the men whenever he had dealings with the Japanese HQ.

• • •

During our time at Adam Park, in the month of September 1942, the Japanese had insisted that all POWs at Changi sign an 'order not to escape'. The order was inspired by an attempted escape by a Corporal Breavington, and several others. They had escaped from Changi and made their way as far as Java before they were recaptured and brought back to Singapore. Cpl. Breavington was admitted to Roberts Barracks Hospital on 10 August 1942 suffering from malaria and other diseases, having lost about 30 kg during the period of his freedom. Breavington, another Australian, and two English officers were taken down to the Changi beach on 8 September and shot. It was reported that Cpl. Breavington had 17 bullets in him before an Indian officer stood over him and put him out of his misery.

The form was specially printed and contained the following particulars:

No. . . . .
I, the undersigned, hereby solemnly swear on my honour that I will not, under any circumstances, attempt escape.
   Signed
   Dated
   At
Nationality
Rank or Position

When this order was issued, the men automatically refused. The Japanese were informed why it was impossible for the men to sign such an order. Protests made by Colonel Galleghan of the AIF and Colonel Holmes, Commander of the British Forces, met with little success as the Japanese refused to compromise, pointing out rather sheepishly that as the order had been issued direct from Tokyo they had no power to alter the terms. If the order promising not to escape were not signed within so many hours, all ranks in Changi would be ordered to remove themselves to the Selarang Barrack Square. The men refused to be threatened and the order remained unsigned.

Steps were taken immediately to shift all essentials to the square, in which were to be accommodated 15 000 troops for the Lord only

No.

I, the undersigned, hereby solemnly swear on my honour that I will
not, under any circumstances, attempt escape.

Signed

Dated

At

Nationality

Rank or Position

No. 1 Camp.

Adam Park, Singapore.

13th September, 1942.

By order of Lieut. Col. Oakes:
　　P.O.W. Camp No. 1.

　By order from the Japanese Commander you are required to sign a
form personally not to escape.
　In addition, I have personally satisfied myself that the A.I.F. Commander at Changi has ordered these Japanese instructions to be
obeyed.
　I therefore order you to sign this form in the required manner and I
accept official responsibility for your action.

(signed)　Lieut. Col. Oakes.
A.I.F. Camp Commander.

This is one of the forms the Japanese insisted the POWs sign. The men's
refusal to sign led to the Selarang incident in September 1942.

knew how long. This number did not include the hospital cases, who
were, after a heated discussion, permitted to remain in their own
area a mile away.

1 — BARRACK SQ., SEPT., 1942.

Selarang Square incident.

Details of Selarang Concentration Area

		TOTAL
Ground area	40 455	39 684 sq.yds
Latrines area	771	
Floor space	19 740	
Staircases	504	18 655 sq.yds
Urinals	402	
Columns, etc.	189	
TOTAL	58 399 sq.yds	
Total number of troops in area	14 960	
Area per man (including kitchens)		3.9 sq.yds (or around 3 sq. metres)

From the outset it was realised that it would be a gigantic struggle to prevent dysentery and other diseases from taking their toll on the men in such a confined space. The ground area was approximately three and a half hectares, around three sides of which were the three-storey army barracks. Bore-holes were dug in the middle of the cement barrack square, tents were thrown up to provide shelter for the improvised kitchens, and the whole square with the milling throng gave the appearance of a busy market place in the streets of old London.

Makeshift beds were erected in the barrack buildings, in tiers of three or more where possible, and the men, when they did sleep had to do so in shifts. A visit to the latrines entailed a wait of half an hour or more in a queue and though time was no object in the circumstances, to those suffering from dysentery time was all important, particularly as there was no water with which to wash one's trousers, or to waste on one's body. Dysentery renders a sufferer helpless, and no doubt the prolonged waiting in the queues claimed many victims during those days in the Selarang Square.

Selarang Square was not enclosed by wire, but Japanese sentries were posted at vantage points around the boundaries of the square to prevent anyone from leaving the area. The boys had buried or hidden a few weapons in the camp so that in the event of the Japanese deciding to shoot the men in the square, they would be able to retaliate. They had even mounted and manned a machine gun on the roof of one of the buildings.

The Japanese had apparently decided that as we would not sign the order willingly, they would force our troops into submission by concentrating them in a small area and cutting off supplies indefinitely, realising that the prisoners could not hold out for very long in such circumstances. The following 'special order' issued by Colonel E. B. Holmes, Commander of the British and AIF troops in Changi, on 4 September 1942, explained the situation to all concerned:

> On 30 August, 1942, I, together with my Area Commanders, was summoned to the Conference House, Changi gaol, where I was informed by the representative of Major General Shimpei Fukuye, GOC POW Camps, Malaya, that all prisoners of war in the Changi camp, were to be given forms of 'promise not to escape', and all were to be given an opportunity to sign this form.
>
> By the laws and usages of war, a prisoner of war cannot be required by the power holding him, to give his parole. I pointed this out to the IJA authorities.
>
> I informed the representative that I was not prepared to sign the form, and that I did not consider that any officers or men of Changi camp would be prepared to sign the form.
>
> In accordance with the orders of the Imperial Japanese Army, all prisoners of war were given an opportunity to sign. The result of that opportunity is well known.
>
> On the 1st September, I was informed by the IJA that those personnel who refused to sign the certificate would be subjected to 'measures of severity', and that a refusal to sign would be regarded as a direct refusal to obey an IJA regulation, which the IJA considered necessary to enforce.
>
> Later on the night of 1st/2nd September, I was warned that on the 2nd September, all prisoners of war persisting in the refusal to sign were to move by 1800 hours to Selarang Barrack Square.

I confirmed both on behalf of myself, and in the name of all prisoners of war our refusal to sign.

The move to Selarang Barracks was accomplished successfully on the same afternoon.

I, and the Area Commanders, have been in constant conference with the IJA, and have endeavored, by negotiation, to have the form either abolished or at least modified.

All that I have been able to obtain is that which was originally a demand, accompanied by threats of 'measures of severity', has now been issued as an official order of the Imperial Japanese Army.

During the period of occupation of Selarang Barracks, the conditions in which we have been placed have been under my constant consideration.

This may be briefly described as such that existence therein will result in a very few days in the outbreak of epidemics, and most serious consequences to those under my command and inevitable death to many.

Taking into account the low state of health in which many of us are now, and the need to preserve our forces intact as long as possible, and in the firm conviction that my action, were the circumstances in which we are now living, fully known to them, would meet with the approval of His Majesty's Government, I have felt it my duty to order all prisoners of war to sign the certificate under the duress imposed by the IJA.

I am fully convinced that His Majesty's Government only expects prisoners of war not give their parole where such parole is to be given voluntarily.

This factor can in no circumstances be regarded as applicable in our present condition.

The responsibility for this decision rests with me, and me wholly, and I fully accept it in ordering you to sign.

I wish to record in this order, my deep appreciation of the excellent spirit and good discipline which all ranks have shown in this trying period.

I look to all ranks to continue in good heart, discipline, and morale.

Thank you all for your loyalty and co-operation.

E. B. Holmes,
Col. Comm. British and AIF

Selarang, 4th September 1942

Our commanders succeeded in forcing the Japanese to issue an order compelling us to sign the order not to escape — this technically amounted to duress, and would be looked upon as such by the outside world when the facts became known.

One can fully appreciate the responsibility incumbent upon a few individuals at such a time, when lack of leadership, the loss of

confidence of the men, or the absence of strict discipline would have
meant absolute chaos and disaster.

This was our first big test under the Japanese, and success was
due only to the wonderful morale displayed by the men during the
whole incident. I feel sure that, in the circumstances, the action of
our own commanders in ordering us to sign the form was justified,
and made sincerely and in the best interests of all concerned.

• • •

During the latter part of 1942 a number of POWs who had been
taken in Java and Timor were transferred to Singapore island and
were quartered at Changi when we returned from Adam Park.
These parties consisted of Javanese; Dutch; Americans of the 141st
Regiment AEF; AIF; and marines of USS *Houston* and a few
hundred sailors who were survivors from HMAS *Perth*. Both HMAS
Perth and USS *Houston* had been sunk in the Sunda Straits on 28
February 1942 in a naval engagement with the Japanese fleet. The
details of this engagement make a very interesting story, and were
related on numerous occasions in lectures by officers and men of
HMAS *Perth* and USS *Houston* during our term as POWs.

The 'Yanks' were very popular with our boys; in fact I think the
feeling became mutual as the result of comradeships which sprung
up in Java, when the 'Yankee' sailors arrived at their camp with
nothing more than the clothes in which they had swum ashore. The
Australians in Java, most of whom were members of units such as
the 2/2nd Pioneer Battalion, 2/3rd Machine Gun Battalion, 105
Transport, were fairly well provided for at that stage and immediately offered things such as clothing, cigarettes and food, and
shared whatever else they had.

The Yanks were forever grateful to our boys, and as late as the
end of 1944 I still heard them talking of the treat the Aussies had
given them upon their arrival in camp in Java. Conversely, they
seemed to dislike the attitude of some of the British soldiers and the
Yanks admitted that they found it almost impossible to remain
quartered in the same barracks with British troops for any length of
time without becoming resentful of them.

The Americans were all good sports and keenly interested in their
own national game of baseball. In spite of their small number, they
challenged our Australian teams to several games of baseball and
rugby football during the earlier part of 1943.

The Aussies needed a little more experience in the American
code football to win a match, but invariably our chaps tossed them
when it came to baseball. Under the captaincy of Capt. Ben
Barnett, ex-Australian Test Team wicket-keeper, our boys developed

quite an interest in the game, and unit teams were formed and several competitions held.

So far as our own unit was concerned, we could only muster a team for the Australian rules game, which we continued to play until the medical officers pointed out that, because of our limited diet and the energy we were wasting, plus the increasing number of injuries being incurred, it was as well that the games be discontinued. We were therefore reluctantly compelled to seek recreation in a more suitable form.

The Yanks and others from Java who arrived at Changi in 1942–43 were given a 'raw deal' in the distribution of British Red Cross supplies. When their party, which was referred to as Java Party originally arrived at Changi, they were informed they were considered to be a party 'in transit', as instructions had been received from the IJA to the effect that their party would be stopping in Singapore temporarily only, pending their eventual dispatch to Japan. For that reason, they were not entitled to participate in the distribution of any Red Cross rations.

This ruling seemed rather severe on the fellows from Java, yet the original decision had not been rescinded even after three months when they were still considered to be a party 'in transit'. Actually, the Java party seemed to be given the 'rough end of the stick' most of the time as they received very little, if any, Red Cross rations, were not paid for working for the Japanese in Java, and furthermore up till June 1944 had not received any Red Cross mail. It is hardly to be wondered that they were at times a bit annoyed with their treatment.

The food situation at Changi in the early part of 1943 continued to be a source of anxiety, and the meagre rations of rice, fish (fresh or otherwise), vegetables and tea which the Japanese issued us left a lot of empty feelings during the intervals between meals.

It was surprising what could be done with rice. The evening meals in our unit consisted of rice and a watery vegetable or fish soup, together with four or five 'doovers'. However, no matter what form the evening rice meal took, long before 'lights out' we were all ravenously hungry again and contemplating what we would have been having for breakfast at home instead of burnt ground rice and a cup of tea.

Our lunch generally consisted of plain rice and a watery 'jungle' stew made up from the 'greens' of the sweet potato tops, Malayan spinach, and anything we could collect from the gardens. At times we would not receive any vegetables from the Japanese for several days owing to shipping difficulties (a large proportion of our early issues used to be supplied from Sumatra), and on such occasions we had to rely on our gardens and on the purchase of *tow-gay* and sweet potatoes, which would be bought through camp messing funds, to which all working personnel contributed out of their own meagre pay.

It was found necessary to implement this fund to enable the purchase of whatever supplies were available from Chinese dealers. However, the demand often exceeded the supply, as the Chinese dealers had many calls on their sources of supply, and at such times our meals were very meagre.

Of course, the majority of us realised that the food situation in Malaya was now a very grave problem, and that any reserves there may have been at the fall of Singapore were now almost exhausted. We were well aware that rice and other commodities were being rationed out to the local civilian population in very small quantities, so we could hardly expect our own treatment to be any better.

The lack of vitamin-rich foods aggravated the state of our rapidly deteriorating health. Deficiency diseases were prominent, with ever-increasing numbers of cases of beri-beri, eye weaknesses, 'happy feet' (a form of paralysis), and skin complaints. The subject of proteins, vitamins, calories and so on was not one that would have preoccupied most of us in peace time, but became of vital concern to us as prisoners of war.

There were temporary and permanent cases of blindness in the Roberts Hospital at Changi, for which the medical officers could only recommend rice polishings, yeast, and a small quantity of Marmite (which represented part of the reserve Red Cross supplies) by way of treatment.

5

Japanese deception

In January/February 1943 we were once again kindly permitted to send a 25 word cable, which was to include the names of six prisoners. The dispatch of the cables was delayed and they made a somewhat belated arrival in Australia as much as six months later. Mine was to the Mayor of Coburg in Victoria and included the names of five other Coburg lads.

Life in Changi during January to April 1943 actually became very monotonous to some, but much was due to their own pessimistic outlook of the outcome, and the fact that quite a number suffered from acute lethargy. The work around the camp was not hard, generally consisting of gardening, trailer parties to collect unit rations and fire wood, rice lumping occasionally, and a party of wood choppers which was sent to rubber plantations 2 or 3 km down the main Changi–Singapore road.

During leisure periods one could always find plenty of books of interest in the library or education centre, and in the evenings there were always the concerts or lectures, debates or discussions to attend. As a POW a sense of humour was essential, and like all groups which included Australians there were more than a smattering of dry humourists.

One point in Changi's favour was the fact that there were few Japanese-controlled working parties and most of the work we undertook was for our own benefit, for example the vegetable gardens in our own unit area. Wally Sheldon was in charge of our unit garden, and despite the belief that the soil in Singapore was not conducive to the growing of tomatoes he produced during 1942, and continued to produce, tomatoes up to 250 g in weight. Members of the 4th Motor Transport who were at Changi from 1942–44 should be very grateful to him and his offsiders for the invaluable greens and other vegetables with which he rarely failed to suppy the cook-house.

The concert parties, both British and Australian, staged some marvellous shows with the assistance and experience of quite a few pre-war professional entertainers.

The British certainly had their share of talented performers, their band included some first-class musicians from leading dance bands in England, so it was hardly surprising that their performances were of a high professional standard. Among the Britishers I recall having heard in Changi were Billy Williams, Dennis East and Padre Foster Haig. Billy Williams could almost make a piano talk, and had the type of voice to which one could listen all evening. Everyone's favourite was 'If I only had wings', a catchy little tune about a ground-staff member of the Royal Air Force.

Dennis East was another British artist of repute, and ranked among the finest English violinists at that time. His playing at the Celebrity Concerts at Changi in 1943 was a privilege to hear for all of us who appreciated classical music.

Tickets for the few concerts given by Dennis East, Padre Foster Haig, and two or three others whose names I cannot recall, were always in great demand. Padre Foster Haig, who had a magnificent voice, died on the Burma railway in 1943, but he will forever be remembered by those who met him for his friendship and 'happy-go-lucky' manner.

At Christmas 1942 a modern version of 'Cinderella' was running at the AIF theatre, and it was decided to approach the Japanese with a view to putting on the show at the Changi gaol for the children of the civilian internees.

The Japanese at first agreed to the idea and preparations for the transfer of 'props' to the gaol were made immediately, but at the last moment their earlier approval was withdrawn. The children were of course very disappointed at missing such a treat, but we were really not surprised, as we had become accustomed to the Japanese frequently changing their minds without any apparent reason.

They did, however, allow the toys which the boys had made during their spare time to be sent down to the children at the gaol, and if the few unfinished toys I saw on my return to Changi a few days after Christmas were any example then the children must have been thrilled with the presents from their Father Christmas over the wall.

At least the depressing atmosphere inside Changi gaol, of which we were to have our own experience later, would have temporarily at any rate, been brightened by the happiness of the children during the celebrations at Christmas.

It was a surprise to us to see civilians continuing to be interned in Changi gaol. We had fully expected that the civilian internees would have been permitted repatriation home, but apparently the Japanese had no intention of allowing this to happen. When we were working on the shrine at Adam Park, quite a number of internees from Australia on their way back to Japan visited the shrine to pay tribute to their dead. Yet there seems to have been no reciprocal arrangement to allow British civilians in Malaya to return home.

It was learned that the internees at the Changi gaol were not being paid at all by the Japanese, and it was proposed that a voluntary contribution be made by our boys towards a fund for the civilians and their children. Each pay day a considerable sum was collected for their benefit, sometimes amounting to several hundred dollars.

The concerts grew better with each performance, and it was intimated by the Japanese that they might agree to record several of the shows for later broadcast over their short-wave radio. Naturally, such a broadcast would have been good propaganda for the Japanese, enabling them to present us to the outside world as being contented and well-treated. After a wait of hours for the recording staff and their apparatus on each occasion, several of the shows were eventually ready for broadcasting, but I cannot say whether they were ever heard outside Singapore

• • •

We had been prisoners of war for more than twelve months, but remained hopeful that an Allied victory in the Far East was near at hand. Little did we know at the time just how far off was our release, what we would have to suffer beforehand, or how many of us would not survive to see that longed-for day.

Early in March 1943 it was vaguely rumoured that a party would be leaving Changi very soon, and that its destination would probably be Thailand. Shortly afterwards, a party of 600 Australians (to be known as D Force) were selected, and preparations made for their early departure.

It was understood that the train journey to Thailand would take about five days, that food on the trip would be good, but that the supply of water would present a problem owing to the length of the journey and the fact that the sources of supply along the line could not be guaranteed to be free of disease. We were also led to believe that the food at the final destination would be far better than at Changi (this would not have been difficult!), and some rosy pictures

Apart from small to large working parties sent from Changi to various points of Singapore island or across into the mainland at Johore Bahru, the main forces were:

CYPHER	DATE LEFT CHANGI	NUMBERS	DESTINATION
A Force	14 May 1942	3 000	Burma
B Force	8 July 1942	1 496	Borneo
C Force	16 Aug. 1942	2 200	Japan
D Force	17 March 1943	5 000	Thailand
E Force	28 March 1943	1 000	Borneo
F Force	18/26 April 1943	7 000	Thailand
G Force	26 April 1943	1 000	Japan
H Force	15 May 1943	3 000	Thailand
J Force	16 May 1943	900	Japan

Note: Of the 2496 men sent to Borneo on B and E Forces, six only survived. They escaped from the Sandakan–Renau March, but Herman (Algy) Reither who was a member of our unit, died on the same day members of a Commando Unit arrived to pick them up.

Details of numbers and departure dates of the main forces to leave Changi.

of a land flowing with milk and honey were painted by those said to have seen the initial notice from the Japanese.

D Force duly departed from Changi in March 1943. The scene of departure was one that I shall never forget. The lads were saying their goodbyes to their old cobbers, and promising to get in touch when they returned home to Australia. Many, of course, did not survive the trip to keep their promises, and others returned in 1944 diseased or crippled for life.

Hundreds of those who failed to return now lie buried in shallow graves in the jungles of Thailand, landmarks of a brave struggle between life and death along the Burma Railway.

In less than twelve months, our own unit lost 23 of the total of 48 on D Force, among whom were Ken Foster, Lex Garner, Bill Donegan, Jack O'Connor, Percy Perris and Frank Williams.

Shortly after the departure of D Force instructions were received from the IJA headquarters that a further party, to be known as F Force, would be drafted away early in April and that 3500 Australians would be required, as well as 3500 British troops.

Of course, as was always the case when a working party was suspected, a certain amount of 'duck shoving' went on before the

Dvr. A. T. 'Snowy' Macklin (Died Singapore 21 July 1945).

Dvr J. G. 'Long Tack' Thompson, Malacca, June 1941.

Left to right: *James Boyle, 'Snowy' Macklin, 'Long Tack' Thompson, Malacca, 1941.*

rolls were finally completed, and the usual team of 'bludgers' paraded to the medical officers with complaints that only seemed to surface when a working party was called for. Still, as it turned out, we were probably better off without them as they would have been more of a hindrance than a help in the months that followed.

We were led to believe that we too were being sent to Thailand — to build a railroad, rumour had it — and as with D Force earlier, it was stated that the food would be better than at Changi. Furthermore, there would not be any marching when we reached our destination, but if there were, our personal baggage, mess gear, and medical supplies, would be transported.

The deception naturally encouraged our medical officers to send away men who were more or less ready to be discharged from hospital, in order that they might have an opportunity of restoring some of their lost health and strength, as it was reported that at the end of the journey, eggs, meat, fruit and fish were plentiful. Most of these hospital cases, approximately 20 per cent of the total, did not last more than a few months but one cannot blame the medical officers, who acted in all sincerity.

On the night of 22 April 1943 (Good Friday Eve) our party of 600 prepared to move off from our parade ground, saying the same words to those we were leaving behind: 'Look after yourself Jack', 'Good luck Alf', 'Don't forget to look me up when you get home old timer' — and so on, until it was time for us to wave a final goodbye.

It left me, I know, with a lump in my throat as I said goodbye to my best pals, Jack Thompson and Alf Macklin, two of the finest men ever in Singapore. The three of us had left Aussie together on Good Friday 1941 and had been inseparable ever since. We had come to know one another better than probably our own brothers did, and it was hard leaving them. Jack and Alf had been taken down with dysentery a few weeks before we left, and were thus compelled to remain behind. I was grateful later that neither of them was allowed to come — fate is sometimes kind.

6

F Force:
Singapore to Ban Pong

Nine months of hell we endured 'up north', nine months when life was not worth living, where men gave up the struggle—to die—and thereby spare themselves the agony of having to live. At times I find difficulty in believing that I actually saw, endured, and what is more survived, the ordeals of those nine months.

Over five days five train loads, each carrying 600 Australians, were drafted away. Our train load was the sixth—F6. The remainder of the Australian and British troops were scheduled to leave over the following week in similar batches of 600.

We were crammed into utility trucks, and left Selarang Barracks Square at about 2.50 am on the morning of April 23, our first stop being the main Singapore railway station. After the rolls had been checked for about the fifth time, we were finally allotted the trucks in which we were to travel.

These trucks, enclosed and constructed wholly of steel, and measuring about 4.8 m by 2.4 m were normally used to carry rice. We were literally stuffed into the trucks, 26 men together with all our personal gear, plus cooking utensils required to establish our new camp. Tinned sardines have more room than we did! It was almost impossible to move one way or the other once we had finally settled down, and necessary for everyone to squat in a cramped position using packs as seats.

We knew that a five-day trip lay ahead of us, so the prospects did not look good. We could not even hang anything on the walls or roof in order to relieve the congestion on the floor, though in a few of the trucks a little timber had been used in the construction inside, and the boys wasted no time in hammering nails into the timber to hang up their packs.

*Rice trucks en route from Singapore to Ban Pong. Photograph: The
Australian War Memorial.*

The only ventilation came from two sliding doors, one on either
side of the truck, and the atmosphere became stifling as soon as the
sun rose. At times it became difficult to breathe, especially when
the train was stationary.

We moved off from Singapore at about 7 am, crossing the causeway which joins Singapore to the mainland, and in the process
disproved the stock crack of Happy Harry, the AIF Concert Party
comedian: 'You'll Never Get Off The Island!'. He'll never know
though, just how glad we were to get back!

Space was too valuable to leave the doorways free, so three or
four men at a time would take turns at sitting in the openings, which
naturally blocked the free flow of air for the rest of us. Remember
too, that we were travelling in a country only one degree north of
the Equator. Although we had become acclimatised to the heat
after a few years in the tropics, it was like being in a furnace as the
sun beat down on the steel sides of our trucks.

During the first day we made very little progress. Being rated as
about third-class freight, we were compelled to wait at sidings every
50 or 60 kilometres so that passenger and other freight trains might
pass. At such times the heat became almost unbearable, but it was

no use complaining, and fortunately the chaps in our truck realised this, which made things a lot easier for all concerned.

We had been issued with about a dozen rice and vegetable rissoles and a few rice and coconut biscuits each on leaving Changi, and these were to represent our ration until the Japanese decided to stop and feed us. Fortunately, the natives frequently came alongside the train carrying baskets of bananas, paw-paws, toffees, and so on, and as these were fairly cheap compared with the prices at Changi we bought freely with the few dollars we had been paid on leaving Singapore.

After 8 hours travelling, we had a meal at Gemas. This consisted of rice and a watery vegetable stew, but the Japanese promised us a good meal at our next stop, which we understood would be Kuala Lumpur. This, when we arrived next morning, proved to be another cold jungle stew with a little curry.

Kuala Lumpur is the capital of Malaya, a wealthy industrial centre in the heart of rich tin-mining country. Its pride is the elaborately constructed railway station, which witnessed the strange sight of our boys, naked and partaking of a shower on the platform in the semi-darkness at 4 am.

Sleep, when it came, was fitful. We all tried to catch up on rest during the day, despite the heat, and at night we arranged four sleeping shifts, while eight or nine men at a time sat huddled in the doorways.

We were not allowed to get out of the trucks when the train stopped, so that whenever nature called it was necessary while the train was in motion to squat in the doorway and hold on to the side — no easy feat, believe me!

After more than two days travelling we reached Prai on the Malay peninsula, directly opposite the island of Penang. At Prai we learned that we would be changing trains there before crossing the border into Thailand. Much to our disappointment, we found that the new trucks were identical to those we had just left.

By now, the monotony, hunger and exhaustion were beginning to tell on the men, some of whose tempers were becoming a little frayed. Arguments and fights began to break out at the slightest provocation. Since leaving Singapore we had eaten only four very poor meals in three days. To add to our worries, we found that after crossing the border, the Thai traders would not accept our Malayan currency.

Soon after crossing the border we were forced to wait for about 8 hours at a small siding because we had almost overtaken the earlier trainload of F5 troops. At least the delay afforded us an opportunity of stretching our legs for a while, but as we were miles from nowhere it meant that we had to wait 22 hours for another bite to eat. However, perhaps this was just a sort of trial run, as we then did not see our next meal for another 26 hours. Altogether, I think we received six meals in the 100 hours it took us to travel between Singapore and Ban Pong, which was our destination.

We arrived at Ban Pong on 27 April 1943. It is between 60 and 70 km south-west of Bangkok. We found it to be much the same as any of the Malayan towns, except that all the shops in Ban Pong appeared to be far better stocked with fruit, eggs, tinned foods, clothing and other merchandise than Singapore.

It was nearly midday when we arrived, and there seemed to be plenty of activity about the main street, with signs that here, at any rate, the Japanese occupation had not hindered prosperity. We moved on at a slow pace through the main street and out on to a wide dusty road, along each side of which there stretched for miles a barren waste without a blade of grass or a sign of foliage on the few trees. To me the place appeared to have an eerie atmosphere, even in the heat of midday, especially when we found the dead trees bordering the track to be alive with vultures, squawking and flapping their wings above our heads as though knowing our fate. So this, we thought, is the 'land of milk and honey' at the end of the dry season!

We set our packs down outside our camp, covered in dust, weary, bum-sore and hungry, after our five days and nights of travelling in the comfort of the Singapore to Bangkok express!

Our guards were rushing around in all directions, and the disarrangement to their plans, due to the delayed arrival of Train No. 5, seemed to upset them considerably.

It was when we arrived at Ban Pong camp that we first encountered Consukie Toyama, a comparatively young Korean guard with whom we were unfortunately to have a long association. While we were lined up being checked, Toyama cruised along the line, spitting out a few orders to our officers. Suddenly, he slammed into Major Anderson of the 2/30th Battalion with the steel shaft of a golf stick he was carrying. He also attacked Lieut. Tweedy of the AASC in the same manner and his back suffered as a result for months afterwards.

Toyama proved to be the curse of F Force, and was directly responsible for the loss of hundreds of lives as the result of his cruelty.

After a check parade we were herded into a small area near the entrance to the camp and given tiny tin discs bearing the numbers 1 to 600, and were informed that we would suffer dire consequences if we were to lose them. I lost mine the first night out on the march!

We were then shown to our quarters, which were rudely erected *attap* huts. Before we had time to sit down, we were ordered to unpack our bags and lay out all our gear in readiness for a Japanese kit inspection, and to then move quickly out of the hut. The Japanese were looking for wireless parts, but any parts we did have were hidden too carefully to be discovered in any casual kit inspection. They did, however, find a number of tools, torches, knives and whistles etc. which they confiscated.

I had taken up my position in the hut beside Doug Weldon of Barwon Heads, Victoria. I discovered from him later that his kit contained wireless parts concealed in pineapple tins, which had been neatly cut in half, then soldered and the label put back on the tin. Water bottles had also been treated in this way, and one of the Japanese had assisted on the march in carrying a concertina which contained a collection of wireless parts!

Lunch that day had been prepared by Chinese cooks and was for once very satisfying. We then started thinking about a shower and a shave, but discovered that no such facilities existed. We found that a 6 m well had been dug, but the water drawn up by bucket was both dirty and foul-smelling.

The stench made it quite obvious in which direction the latrines lay. Swarming with flies and crawling with maggots, they consisted of frail bamboo slats acting as a platform on which to squat over a small trench. The conditions were ideal for the spreading of dysentery and enteric diseases, and undoubtedly a number of the later cases emanated from Ban Pong, whose latrines were among the worst I saw along the whole stretch of the railway.

Later that day, we learned to our horror that we still had 300 km to travel before reaching our final destination, and that furthermore the trip was to be done 'on foot'! Naturally this came as a great shock, and we immediately began to wonder how on earth those among us who had been discharged from hospital to join the party were going to make the journey.

The Japanese pointed out that the few who were allowed to stay at Ban Pong would be sent on in a few days: they would still have to march no matter how sick they were. We wondered to ourselves why the Japanese had not sent us all by train over the 150 km or so of rail that had already been laid, especially when it appeared that completion of their railway between Thailand and Burma was a matter of some urgency!

Major Anderson advised us all to lighten our packs as much as possible, and to dispose of any surplus clothing. Fortunately we found this to be both simple and profitable, as the Thais were only too willing to buy anything—from a toothbrush to a typewriter.

The money we received enabled us to buy paw-paws, bananas, eggs and tomatoes, a welcome change from our normal diet.

Unfortunately we were not at Ban Pong long enough for the food to make any material difference to our state of health. We moved out on the night of April 28, and so began the long march to the Burma border.

Transcription of the shorthand diary kept by James Boyle from 23 April to 14 December 1943

Left Changi camp at about 2.30 Good Friday morning, 23rd April by utility truck for Singapore station. Were put in railway trucks 26 men to truck (16' × 8') together with gear, no ventilation, besides door. Very little room for each man. Necessary to sleep during day and in shifts at night, extremely hot.

Meals very few and far between. Five meals in 100 hours. Without a meal for 22 and 26 hours respectively. Fortunately able to buy a few bananas and paw paws at stations, but money of no use once in Thailand. Very fatiguing and men very discontented after five days journey.

Had a shower in nude on Kuala Lumpur station and Ipoh. Very bad latrine facilities. Did P. T. one morning. Train very slow and stops for first day or so very frequent, making carriage stifling.

Very uninteresting trip, and up to that point one of the worst experiences of my life.

Calls of nature fore or aft necessary sit in door way and hold on to side of door. Very difficult procedure.

Played banjo at several stops. Arrived Ban Pong station 27th April.

Ban Pong—marched a mile with gear to camp. Japanese very nasty. This where we first encountered Toyama, the golf stick merchant who bashed up Major Johnson of the 2/30th battalion and Lieut. Tweedy, who had trouble with his back for a long time afterwards. His first working party since POW.

Put in huts without floor and kit inspection immediately in huts. Given numbers (90). Had mess parade. Drew water from filthy well by means of a bucket and rope—stinking water.

Given instructions that would be marching 140 miles so advisable to get rid of all possible gear. Sold shorts, shirts, pyjamas, singlets, etc. Bought eggs, bananas and got a case of meat and vegetable.

Lavatories absolutely shocking and things generally very bad from medical point of view.

Not feeling very enamoured of a good working party.

Ban Pong (to Tama Kam)—16 7/8 miles.

Left Ban Pong at about 11.30 p.m. on 28th April with all gear (pack on back and kit bag strapped on pole with 'Chicken' Smallhorn's gear).

Horrible experience, men falling out after a few miles from exhaustion and cobbers carrying their gear and others helping them along. Men all along track limping through bad footwear blisters etc. and fainting, stomach troubles.

7

The long march

I n accordance with Major Anderson's advice, we had all lightened our packs considerably in preparation for the long march. Nevertheless, by the time we made our very first stop along the track many additional articles suddenly became dispensable. Even cherished souvenirs of home and loved ones had to be abandoned.

'Chicken' Smallhorn, ex-Fitzroy footballer and Victorian Brownlow Medallist, and I decided to strap our extra packs to a bamboo pole, and carry it between us on rubber pads on our shoulders. The idea proved quite successful.

Our party had not progressed more than a few kilometres along the road out of Ban Pong before men were calling for assistance with their kit, and others were falling out by the roadside in a faint. Throughout the night, cries of help were passed on down the column—'Man out in No. 5 Company', 'Man out in No. 2 Company', 'Stretcher bearers required at rear', until the calls seemed to become part of the night.

Every two or three kilometres it would be necessary to give the men a spell to allow the stragglers to catch up with the main column, while others who were absolutely worn out were somehow sent on by bus.

We had two medical officers in F6; one was Major 'Buck' Rogers, the other's name now eludes me. All night long they dashed backwards and forwards from one end of the column to the other in answer to calls for a doctor, so that by the end of the night's march they must have walked almost twice as far as anyone else, carrying their own packs of which they steadfastly refused to be relieved.

A number of Thais followed us along the road for a while, until we discovered they were seeking to pilfer what they could. A few well-aimed kicks soon dissuaded them. Some nights later however some unfortunates, including Dave Cupples of our unit, were relieved of practically all they possessed, when Thais raided our baggage trucks.

As dawn broke, the pitiful sight of our struggling column was one I shall never forget. The men were strung out for miles along the track, their faces haggard, their shoulders drawn under the weight of their packs. Dozens were limping from blistered and sore feet, whilst others carried their boots in their hands.

Seeing the condition of the men in the light of early morning, our officers decided to halt the party until the stragglers caught up, and to wait until everyone had a good hour's rest before completing the remainder of the 28 km to our first camp—Tama Kam.

One officer, Major Anderson 2/30th Batt. sold his own watch to hire a few rickshaws so that several of the worst cases might be carried. The sun was well up in the sky by the time the first camp hove into sight, and the thought that there lay a rest on reaching it, installed new spirit into the men. One poor old chap who had struggled on in spite of his age and condition, made a supreme effort and then fell flat on his face just inside the camp gate, and lay on the ground thoroughly exhausted like some Olympic athlete completing a marathon.

He obviously would not give up until he had completed the journey.

After a short *tenko*, we lost no time in seeking out some large trees where we might sleep for a while before moving on that night. However, blistered feet required attention, and we had also to eat to maintain our strength, despite our desire to sleep. Fortunately, food from the native canteen was plentiful, and the coffee the most enjoyable drink I had tasted since the fall of Singapore. We fared very well on eggs, fruit, biscuits and cakes.

Soon after the evening mess parade, we were ordered on parade and informed that we were to move off to our next camp, 25 km away. We were relieved to hear that for a cost of 50 cents each our gear would be transported in yak carts to the next camp. The job of looking after the baggage, plus a ride in the truck, was offered to me but as I was not feeling too bad really I suggested that Chicken should go, as he had only just been discharged from Changi hospital after an appendix operation.

We waited on the parade ground for hours, and were finally informed that owing to a report of an alleged knifing of a Japanese guard by a Thai further up the track, it was possible we might not be moving on that night. Still we had to wait, and about midnight we commenced the next stage of our march.

After the first few hours I had trouble keeping my eyes open, and found myself wandering off the road, so I decided to hold on to the haversack straps of Billy Cook (another member of our unit) and close my eyes altogether. In that fashion I was at least able to rest them. We then took turn about marching in this way, and others did the same.

In spite of the fact that we had little gear to carry, apart from stretchers, buckets, mess containers and the like, many of the men were so weak that they soon began to fall out, unable to go any further. Some we helped along as best we could, others had to be carried on stretchers and this was no easy task. It was only sheer determination, and a wish to show the Japanese that they could not break our spirit that kept us going.

We made Kamburei at about 9 am 30 April 1943, and learned that we would be camped there for 36 hours. There were no huts with the exception of a small RAP (regimental aid post) which was crowded out with malaria, dysentery, and other cases, so we had to seek covering in the nearby scrub. After breakfast, we erected rough shelters out of a few branches, lay down, and were soon sleeping soundly.

We were again troubled by Thais stealing any unguarded gear. A party of about six of us had prepared our makeshift covering in the scrub, and while we were preparing a fire a Thai was seen running off with Fred McBean's pack. Fred McBean and I gave chase and after 150 m or so the Thai dropped the pack, when we had almost caught up to him. Others, however, were not so lucky.

During the afternoon it began to pour with rain. Fortunately Sgt. 'Oscar' Wiles, who had transferred to our unit to join F Force, had discovered a small *attap* shed, so as many as possible of our chaps transferred to this very welcome shelter for the night. Oscar arrived back before we were awake next morning with omelettes, cakes, and coffee, which he had bought from the owner of the hut.

We made the acquaintance of our host later in the morning, and succeeded in selling him surplus clothing, pens, etc. He seemed to take a fancy to my mandolin, so although I was loathe to part with it, I let him have it rather than lug it any further. We were grateful to this Thai, and I'm sure he would have paid had the Japanese found out that he had offered us his hospitality.

During the morning we marched down the road about 2 km to the town, where we underwent tests by Japanese doctors for malaria and dysentery. This was our first experience of a Japanese dysentery test, which involved inserting a glass or bamboo rod none too gently into the anus! The same method was used to detect cholera victims and carriers.

Kamburei was referred to as the 'dry camp' because the only sources of water were the river, which lay 2 km away, and a well at a nearby native hut, for which the owner charged at the rate of 5 cents a bucket. Our washes therefore were few and far between. It was recommended by our medical officers that any water we drank should either be boiled or treated with chloride of lime. Water became a very serious problem during the 300 km march, as we were reluctant to wash in, let along drink, any creek or river water upon which we knew the natives to have kampongs.

However, so far as train 6 of F Force was concerned, Kamburei could have been referred to as 'wet camp', as it again started to rain during the second afternoon, so we again sought the shelter of our friend's hut until it was near time to parade for mess. When we emerged, we found the flat ground more like a small lake, the RAP patients washed out, and the open-air cookhouse an entire failure. The evening's rice and stew now contained more water and mud than usual, and the doctors condemned it.

Just as dusk was falling we were ordered out on parade to commence the next stage of our march, with the rain still pouring down. But we didn't hear the familiar cry of 'Prepare to move' until about 11.30 pm, because one of the Japanese guards claimed someone had stolen his watch! In the meantime, we stood out in the rain but could not sit down, nor set our packs down, as the parade ground was completely under water.

• • •

When we were at last able to make a move, the ordeal which followed proved to be one of the worst we experienced on the march. The road between Ban Pong and Kamburei had been bitumen, but as soon as we passed the outskirts of Kamburei, we moved off onto a jungle track, where we trudged through mud and water almost knee-deep at times. Men were continually falling head-first into holes along the track, emerging covered in mud and slush from head to foot, or slipping and sliding on the treacherous stretches of the higher ground. It was a pitch-black night, further intensified by the thick growth of overhanging trees, bamboo and creepers of the thick jungle through which we were passing.

The rain continued to pelt down in torrents, as it does in the tropics during the approaching monsoons, and this was accompanied by terrific claps of thunder and vivid flashes of lightning, which momentarily blinded us. Our nerves were on edge the whole time, as the dark was so intense that it was impossible for the eyes to make out the outline of the track, so that at any sudden turn someone would wander off and stumble into a ditch or over the stump of a tree.

We came across several Japanese trucks, which had become bogged. Others that tried to pull them out failed, and finished up in the same plight.

We tried tying something white—a piece of cloth, a mug—to the backs of our packs, but to no avail. Holding on to the pack of the fellow in front was of no use either, as it meant two trying to keep their feet and usually ended with both toppling in the mud. We had 24 km to march before our next camp, so tried to make the best of it.

The boots I had been issued before leaving Changi had become more a nuisance than benefit, as the loose nails in the soles were piercing my feet at every step, so I was quite relieved when I put my foot in a particularly deep muddy hole and my boot came out minus the whole sole. I continued in my stockinged feet. Lots of the chaps had already worn out their boots, and were having trouble staying upright on the slippery surface—I joined them as soon as I took to bare feet.

Around 5 am we rested for two hours, and ate our haversack ration of cold plain rice and a small piece of dry salted fish. Bamboo fires were lit along the track, and they lent a sorrowful light to the picture of a wet and weary body of men whose unshaven, mud-bespattered faces registered looks of forlorn hope and wonderment. The two hours rest was very welcome and toward morning as the rain eased off we found the going a lot easier. The men were, however, almost completely exhausted after a gruelling night.

The main body, which was also carrying the stretcher cases, reached Temple camp—Wampoh—at about 10 am on 2 May 1943, but the remainder of the party hobbled and limped in for several hours afterwards. This camp was situated on the edge of a wide, swift-flowing river. We lost no time in refreshing ourselves in its cool waters, and washing out our mud-spattered clothing. We then drew our breakfast from the cook-house and sought the shelter of the scrub to rest before moving on that night.

I made efforts to secure some sort of footwear before evening, and located a chap with two old boots from which the toes had been cut by someone who had found them too small. I accepted them only too eagerly, and they served me well for the remainder of our long march.

On the next stage of the march we were once again able to arrange for transport of our packs, but the convenience resulted in a number of chaps losing every bit of gear they possessed. One Yi Camp was 100 km from Ban Pong, and we reached it after five nights, which, taking into account our 36 hours rest at Kamburei, was not a bad effort, considering the conditions. One Yi camp covered quite a large area and as with most camps along the track it was set within a short walking distance of a river, over which a large wooden bridge had been constructed.

We found one of our mates of the 8th Div. Sigs, Sgt. 'Curly' Meakin, in charge of the cook-house and although Curly probably had not even made a cup of tea before the war, the food that came out of his cook-house at One Yi was better than any we had received along the track up to that time.

At each camp, several of our small party—'Oscar' Wiles, Pat Byrne, Billy Cook, Lloyd Hoarse, Junior Johnson, Chicken Smallhorn and myself—would erect a makeshift covering against the rain, while others investigated what could be 'scrounged' around the camp or bought from the natives. We had pooled our resources at Ban Pong and had found that in this manner our money lasted longer and we were able to help one another when the need arose.

A complete rest at One Yi for a further 36 hours gave us renewed strength, and we moved on toward our destination—the Burma border—which we understood was still another 200 km.

By this time we were beginning to leave civilisation behind, and saw few signs of habitation. The track was bordered on either side by thick creeping vines and bamboo which rose into the air for 10 or 15 metres, and the only sounds that penetrated the still night apart from marching feet were the cries of monkeys the size of orang-outangs. Wild banana palms, whose enormous leaves were sometimes 2 m in length and .5 m in width were sprinkled along the track, and we found them to be useful coverings for our head and shoulders when it rained.

As we left One Yi we crossed the main river, and learned that a large number of Japanese troops and their supplies were sent up river by barges as far as possible toward the Burma border, thence to continue by foot to the west coast. The road over which we travelled was said to have been used by caravan trains and merchants trading between Thailand and Burma centuries ago. We guessed that the roads would be impassable during the monsoons unless heavy repair work was undertaken immediately.

The distance between One Yi and Tahsao was a matter of 24 km and I for one found it to be one of the most arduous stretches of the trip. In addition to lumping our own gear, there was an increasing number of stretcher cases and disabled who needed help. At one stage, although our team had just been relieved, Billy Cook, Lloyd Hoarse, 'Oscar' Wiles and I offered to take over the transport of a stretcher case. We thought that Tahsao could not be too far distant, but we must have covered almost another 3 km before we sighted it.

By that time I was almost a stretcher case myself, and the others feeling the same.

In my opinion, many POWs were foolish in their readiness to volunteer for any task that needed doing. In the end, some of these chaps realised when it was too late that they were exceeding their strength, and so succumbed to the many diseases waiting to pounce on the weakened victim.

As we marched into Tahsao camp we passed a neat and recently made little graveyard, set back off the road among the trees and bamboo and bordered by a low bamboo fence. A small wooden cross had been erected over each grave. To our amazement, we learned that there had been 21 deaths in 17 days among the members of D Force camped there. It was to us a major tragedy.

Tahsao, a base camp, was better equipped than most to accommodate troops, though our party was not given any shelter while we were there. D Force chaps were accommodated in *attap* huts. There was quite a large maintenance and repair workshop for Japanese vehicles, and in one sector we found a small hospital to which the worst cases from D Force were sent from along their section of the railway.

The railway line had already been laid as far as Tahsao when we arrived, so once again it might have seemed sensible for the Japanese to have allowed us to travel that far by train, thereby saving us a 123 km march.

Since at Tahsao there were adequate medical supplies to treat cases of dysentery, malaria, etc. with roofed *attap* huts not previously encountered along the track, it was deemed expedient to approach the Japanese to leave as many sick as possible here for a few days.

The Japanese, however, would not hear of the idea, and ordered all but the few *they* considered unable to move, out on to the track the same evening. They bashed with bamboo sticks the sick who were slow in obeying. Dozens of the men were suffering from active dysentery, or were in a high state of fever. Others were hobbling tenderly on blistered and ulcerated feet, and all of us were weakened through lack of adequate food and sufficient rest.

• • •

We carried on as though in a stupor, our eyes staring fixedly on the ground in front of us, mindless of our surroundings except to follow the lagging step of the fellow in front. We had long since lost the feel of our legs. When, after a couple of kilometres, the cry of 'resto' would be heard, we would flop down where we stopped, sometimes without even bothering to remove our packs. Sleep was almost instantaneous. Though the stop might be for ten minutes only, on the hard road or in a pool of mud, the rest was like a whole night's sleep on a soft spring mattress.

Our slumbers were invariably disturbed by the ever too soon order of 'Pick up gear—Prepare to move', and once again we would trudge on through the night. The hours just before dawn were always the worst. Chaps would fall asleep whilst marching, only to be rudely awakened when they stumbled into the scrub on the side of the track. One unfortunate, who in spite of his age had somehow kept up with Party 6, fell asleep during a 'resto' and apparently failed to waken when the order came to move. His absence remained unnoticed until *tenko* was called on our arrival at the next camp, when a guard was sent back to find him.

The next stage of our journey took us through very rugged mountainous country for about 40 km, and the Japanese proposal to lay a railway line through such terrain was obviously a gigantic undertaking. It was in this vicinity that H Force, the one following our own, was sent to work, and their task must have been an unenviable one.

We completed the march through the mountains in two stages: the first to Rintin, the second to Hindato. We reached Rintin, 165 km from Ban Pong, on 7 May 1943, and discovered that a large number of Australian and Dutch troops—members of D Force— were camped there, but to our disappointment learned that those of our own unit who were on D Force had moved out of the camp that same morning. A few of our chaps, who were in hospital, remained behind and from them we learned of the conditions under which they were working and living along the line, and what they thought of the Japanese and their railway!

During the morning one chap from our own unit, Sgt. Stan Redman of South Australia, died of a collapsed bowel. Of the others, some were hardly recognisable as those who had left Changi a few weeks before our own force. Their faces were hollow and drawn, their eyes sunk back into their heads, and their still bodies flat on the bamboo slats were little more than skin and bone. They explained in voices little more than whispers that they had suffered severe attacks of dysentery and malaria. The medical staff could do little with their scant supply of medication. Four of our unit on D Force had already died, and were buried in the small graveyard nearby.

Much to my horror, I was suddenly stricken during the night with a violent attack of vomiting and diarrhoea. The first attack came on me so soon after midnight that I barely had time to clear our makeshift shelter, before I began to discharge from both ends.

Every half hour or so I would have to crawl out over the others and make a dash in the dark until by dawn I no longer had the strength to stand or squat, and had to lie on the ground and let things take their course.

After the boys had eaten their breakfast. 'Oscar' Wiles piggy-backed me over to sick parade, where a Eurasian medical officer kindly issued me with six M&B tablets, with instructions that I remain at Rintin for 24 hours. My recovery after taking the M&Bs was however so rapid and welcome that I endeavoured to persuade the MO to allow me to go on with F6 that evening, but he explained that this would be unwise after such a severe attack of possible dysentery. One of our own unit pals, Bill Donegan, a member of D Force had died of the same disease at Rintin on April 19. I had come to know poor old 'Donny' pretty well at Adam Park, and the news of his death came as a great shock to me.

The next stage of our march—22 km—took us to Hindato. Fortunately I had the company of three good pals of our own unit in Doug Dawson of Manjimup, Western Australia, Pearce Graham and Fred McBean. My shorthand diary records that we had a fairly good trip, and that Hindato had a very welcome cold stream close to the camp.

At our next stop, we encountered a Japanese sergeant who seemed to be 'regimental happy'. He will no doubt be remembered by those who passed through Princala for his mess parades where he insisted on the men forming up in eight long lines, the head man of which would stand back about ten paces until his turn came to move up to one of the eight mess orderlies dishing out the tucker.

From Hindato we moved to Princala. Having now slipped back to F7, I found myself, rather unhappily I am afraid, attached to the first bunch of F Force Pommies. I was not impressed with the attitudes or standard of discipline of many of these members of the British Army, and I found the atmosphere on the rest of the march to be entirely different from that in F6. Strange as it may seem, the Pommies refused even to carry their own kitchen buckets and mess dixies. Admittedly this extra weight entailed hardships in the short term, but the refusal meant they were short of essential cooking utensils later on.

We reached the 227 km camp on May 13, and found some D Force boys constructing a huge wooden bridge near the camp. They were fortunately assisted in their labours by the services of an elephant which was hauling the huge logs into position.

We found the food at Taganon a little more varied than was usual. All troops received an issue of dried fish, and the sicker men in the temporary hospital were given specially cooked meals. We all had a good rest during the day and moved out of camp in the late afternoon, leaving behind Jimmy Farrell of our unit who had, I think, contracted a dose of dysentery—which left him too weak to withstand an attack of cholera a few days later at Nicki.

By this time we had little left of the money from our sales at Ban Pong, but at Tampura we managed to rake up amongst our gear a surplus towel, for which a native offered us a bunch of eighteen bananas in exchange. It was my last taste of a banana for eight months. At this camp, the Japanese made certain that we did not wash ourselves in the river anywhere near their own washing place, no doubt for fear of our infecting the water.

After a short march of 20 km to Tamarau we came on members of the 2/29th Infantry Battalion, who had left a few days prior to our departure from Changi.

May 1943

Moved out on 19th May to next camp. About six miles distance between two camps.

Sick again at this camp and sat up for three hours vomiting.

From Ban Pong to Shimo Sonkurei—188¾ miles.

Shimo Sonkurei. Arrived at next camp and found rest of our unit here. Also remainder of other units in earlier trains. Billetted in huts without roofs. Surprised to find Toyama here. Given tents but insufficient to cover twenty men and started to rain in afternoon and mud all over the place and everything wet. Conditions absolutely terrible and looks like being a very trying time from now on.

Cholera outbreak also at this camp.

No water available unless boiled. Small creek ordered out of bounds so unable to wash.

Arrived here on 20th May, 1943. During night rained and nearly all bamboo floors collapsed.

Went out to work on 21st May on railway and worked till 9.30 and started to rain again.

Cholera still bad here and further nine cases on 23rd. Had to work all through day in rain, very cold and miserable and men look like cracking up under strain. Conditions terrible.

On 24th May only about 60 men available out of 163. Received another cholera inoculation. Three more deaths. Railway work abandoned on 23rd because of rain, so employed on road for two days.

Food pretty crook but fair considering fact that cookhouse out in rain.

Now been raining for five days continuously and clothes all wet, socks full of mud and boots cut and falling to bits. Hundreds of men already going out to work without boots.

30/5/43. Holiday today or rather men stayed in camp. As a result of very forceful letter written by Major Hunt and Major Johnson to Japanese regarding cholera situation here and the treatment which had been meted out to us during the trip up, and the state and present condition of our camp.

Asked that the letter be sent to International Red Cross at Bangkok or Rangoon and likened out treatment to that of slaves.

Up to date over 40 deaths due to cholera, including Bert Chandler WX of our unit on 29/5/43. Ninety seven cases of suspected cholera still in hospital, but camp still in very bad state.

8

Cholera

After the usual check parade on our arrival at Tamarau we were herded past a row of huts occupied by Chinese, Tamils, Malays, and probably a few Burmese, and for the first time on our march, we were agreeably surprised to see that there were a few luxurious bamboo huts for us to occupy, with floors too! Of course, the huts didn't have any roofs, but that was a mere detail. We all thoroughly enjoyed the bamboo slats under our backs, which were at least a welcome change from the damp ground.

We learned from the natives who were also being employed along the railway line, that many of them too were dying daily from tropical diseases. The majority of them had been rounded up in Malaya and sent to these unpaid forced labour camps. It would be an impossibility to estimate accurately how many thousands of these civilians died on the Burma railway.

There was a great rumpus during the afternoon of our stay at Tamarau when it was discovered that a pair of boots had been stolen from an officer of the 2/29th Battalion A.I.F. All of our party were ordered out on parade, and a kit inspection found the boots to have been taken by a Pommie in our party. Boots were, of course, at a premium and if the officer had two pairs he deserved to lose one pair, as in all probability the soldier had none at all!

Thieving was fairly prevalent in established camps all along the line, but I would not say any of the culprits suffered from kleptomania. I tried it myself on several occasions when I found the Japanese to have something which I considered I could put to better use. However, thieving from one of your own mates was an entirely different matter, and any offenders when caught were dealt with severely.

One of my most memorable experiences of the 320 km march took place soon after our departure from Tamarau, in the late evening of 15 May 1943. We were marching on a wide track in comparatively open country. To the right, a few hundred metres back from the road, a steep hill rose to the darkening sky; the sun was just setting, directly ahead of us. Our small party of F6 AIF hangers-on had been sent to the rear of the column of F7. We were at that stage marching down a slight incline and could see the remainder of the long column stretched out for several hundred metres in front of us.

All of a sudden, as if from nowhere, there sounded the first few blasts of 'Retreat', and every man in the column stopped dead in his tracks. Not a man, apart from the Japanese guards, moved a step forward until the bugler, who was obviously from a camp a little further along the road, had blown his last note. No bugler could have sounded the call to a more silent body of men, or imagined that it could have had such an effect on their morale. Their bearing and spirit changed almost instantaneously; in fact one almost expected a rousing three cheers for 'King and Country'!

Beating Retreat at sunset is an army tradition dating back to 1690. Later, in 1779, Retreat is described as 'a beat of drums, the trumpets at the same time sounding at the head of their troops'. In any camp throughout the British Empire soldiers always observe a 'stand fast' at the sounding of Retreat at sunset, and the tradition is retained in Queen's Regulations today.

• • •

Our march from Tamarau to Nicki camp was our fourth night without a rest, and naturally we were dog-tired. We met up once again with our own boys from F6 at Nicki, and learned from them that although the camp was on the whole a good one, the water supply was bad as the small creek running through the camp was not more than a few inches deep.

Nicki was the last staging camp before we reached our final destination. It had been established to accommodate a working party from F Force, so that the cookhouse was better equipped than most. On the very next day, however, we found that the rice issue had been cut down.

The doctors here had discovered six cases of suspected cholera among the sick in the hospital hut. Apart from these quite a few others were dangerously ill, mostly with dysentery and malaria. On May 16, the day of our arrival at Nicki, we lost the first member of F Force. He was one of the 2/29th Battalion party which had arrived a few days earlier, and soon after his arrival he was removed to the isolation hut where he died.

The doctors and men were becoming alarmed at the possibility of a cholera outbreak. Fortunately, on the morning after our arrival the medical panniers arrived from Ban Pong and the doctors lost no time in preparing for our first cholera inoculation. We learned however, that one inoculation was not sufficient to combat this dreaded and comparatively unknown disease — we lost five men within 36 hours.

One can imagine how the men felt in the tense atmosphere that surrounded the camp during those first few days, with death hanging over the heads of every one of us. Twenty-four hours before, the men who now lay cold up on the hill had been walking about the camp as normally as any of us. Those who contracted cholera during the period between the first and second inoculations were usually dead within 48 hours.

It was decided that we would remain at Nicki for two of three days before moving on to Shimo Sonkurai. During the afternoon of our second day Fred McBean, Doug Dawson and I were sitting on the bamboo slat floor of our hut chatting. This had been our first real opportunity to sit and think. At such times, one's thoughts always turned to home, and one wondered how our loved ones would feel had they but known of our whereabouts and the conditions under which we were living.

Poor old Fred was sitting there bemoaning the fact that he had nothing to smoke. I delved down into my pack and unearthed a battered pipe. I'd given up smoking soon after Singapore fell, as tobacco was too dear and food was a far more important item to liquidate the few cents the Japanese paid us.

Fred just sat there sucking away at the stem of the pipe imagining for all the world he was smoking a bowlful of the choicest Virginian leaf.

It was during the afternoon of our second day at Nicki that I decided to record in shorthand the events of the past few weeks. From that day until I returned to Singapore at the end of 1943, I recorded day by day the main happenings of our camp. I would take my little notebook out to work on the railway, concealing it from the Korean guards and Japanese engineers, and make a few entries during our lunch break. It was hardly ever possible to make a note in camp when on an outside working party, as invariably we left before sunrise and got back to camp after nightfall.

On some days my notes were recorded in purple ink made from indelible pencil, and other times they were written in a very pale solution of mercurochrome from the RAP, but mostly I had to fall back on the stump of an old pencil. Strangely enough my little note book was sufficient to within about two pages to make a daily recording right up to the time we returned to Singapore in December 1943.

The Lord only knows what would have happened to me and my diary if it had been found during the many kit inspections the Japanese made. Naturally I hid my diary and notes whenever we had warning of these inspections, but in the end I had to bury them for nine months under a hut at our Orchard Road Camp, Singapore. After our liberation in August 1945, I went back to this camp only to find that the huts had been removed. Fortunately, I had measured distances from certain spots, and was able to unearth my treasured possessions — in as good a condition as the day I had buried them. I had wrapped the notes in old sticky gas-cape inside a soldered tin container. 'Judge' Wilde, who had accompanied me to recover some of his own papers, was not so lucky — his had been reduced to a sodden mass of pulp.

• • •

Cholera was at that stage of our imprisonment as yet an unknown quantity, but I made my first contact with one of its victims on the morning of our third day at Nicki. I had gone to the hospital hut to see the medical officer as once again I had been up for three hours during the night, vomiting my insides out. It transpired that my condition was due only to extreme debility, but I was terrified and feared the worst until I was reassured by the medical officer at Nicki, and was given some medicine to help me keep my meagre ration where it belonged.

As I was about to walk back through the *attap* hut one of the English medical orderlies came in carrying a patient in his arms. No sooner had they entered the hut than the tell-tale rice water began to flow from the victim, leaving a trail of whitish-looking fluid in his path.

Major Stevens, the camp's senior Australian medical officer, soon left little doubt in my mind as to the serious nature of his patient's condition. Major Stevens had apparently issued instructions to the medical orderlies that the man was to be left outside the hut until a proper examination could be conducted. He was furious at having had his orders disobeyed, but the damage had already been done.

The patient was laid out on the dirt floor of the hut and a receptacle of some sort placed where he needed it most. The medical orderly who was the subject of Major Steven's wrath immediately proceeded to cover up the trail of the disease, as the green-backed flies would soon have discovered the mess in which to dabble their feet. Our party left Nicki early next morning, so I do not know whether or not the man survived.

We moved out on May 19 and after a march of 10 km reached
Shimo Sonkurai, which was to be our camp for the next three
months. We had covered 304 km in exactly three weeks since
leaving Ban Pong. It was a feat of which everyone who completed
the journey — in any condition, half-dead or otherwise — could feel
justly proud.

May–June

The situation through which we were now passing was one which would go down in history of the AIF, and Major Hunt pointed out that the treatment we were receiving should not be given to prisoners of war but was only for slaves.

Pearce Graham discharged from cholera ward today and feeling much better. Six more deaths on 30th up to five o'clock.

31/5/43. Received news on parade in morning that five or six men had 'gone through'.

Only 300 men required for work party this morning.

Men later recalled to camp after Japanese being approached by Major Hunt demanding their return to camp.

Worked in morning cutting bamboo.

Fifty-three deaths from cholera up to 12 o'clock midday.

Very wet day.

Pearce Graham much better.

Three yaks being cooked for tea tonight.

Men still looking very dirty, clothes almost in rags, unshaven, impossible to get sufficient water to wash. Boots worn out. No dry clothing.

Men losing weight through lack of good food. Hopeful that some consideration will be given to letter as rumour that about 800 cases of cholera amongst those on the whole road.

No doubt that it is impossible for troops to stay in this area as apparently whole atmosphere infected with disease. Japanese issue of quinine tablets insufficient in strength to stop malaria as plenty of cases being admitted to hospital.

1/6/43. Woke in morning with finger badly swollen and apparently infected.

Worked on bamboo party then went on sick parade. Given no duties and feeling of oncoming dengue or 'flu.

Sixty deaths from cholera up to midday.

Still raining and camp very muddy and in bad state.

All dysentery and diarrhoea cases transferred to another hut.

2/6/43. On no duties today but feeling much better. Lay down during morning and went on sick parade — given light duties.

Seventy deaths up to midday, but only a few admissions, and according to reports patients all feeling brighter and happier.

Work party out today.

Peter Bellairs down with 'flu.

Dozens of men still reporting on sick parade — and still raining most of time. Conditions bad and very muddy. Food a little better.

9

Shimo Sonkurei camp

On arriving at Shimo Sonkurei we marched through the camp gates, passed the Korean guard and lined up for the inevitable Japanese *tenko*. Imagine our consternation to see standing before the parade, our old adversary of the golf-stick — Toyama! We had become used to all sorts of bad luck, but not that bad.

After we were dismissed from the parade, our company was led to the huts we were to occupy. Ours was the one furthest from the parade ground, and the further we walked the worse the huts became. Two sections of our hut were without any roof at all, and the sides were leaning at such crazy angles that it came as no surprise when most of the sides and floor collapsed during the first night.

The huts were constructed of the usual split bamboo, the joins laced together with vine fibre. Built properly, these huts were quite substantial, but ours appeared to have been built without the services of any building inspector.

Except that we were given a number of canvas tarpaulins to arrange over us as covers, we would probably have been better off outside on the ground. The floors of the huts, made of split bamboo and a little under a metre off the ground, ran along each side of the hut with an earthen floor in the centre. Bamboo uprights divided the slat floors into bays in which twenty men were crammed with all their odds and ends of gear.

We had no sooner made the most of our available tarpaulin covers than we experienced the heralding of the monsoons with a torrential downpour. In less time that it takes to write these few words, we looked like drowned rats and all of our kits and bedding were a sodden mass. The tiny drains running through under the bamboo floors soon became small creeks as the water swept down from the steep hill at the back of the camp. The pathway through the hut quickly became a quagmire as the rain pelted down. It continued to rain all afternoon and most of the night of May 20, and nearly all the bamboo floors collapsed under the weight of the men.

During the first night we were continually being awakened by the screams of some men, and the disturbance of others being carted away to hospital. Three of the twenty men in our bay, amongst whom was Percy Graham from Traralgon in Gippsland, were stricken with cholera during the first night and were carted off through the rain to Cholera Hill, up over the creek at the west end of the camp.

We could see the flares of the big fires burning furiously up on the hill, despite the rain. The stricken victims required as much saline drip as it was possible to give them, and the water for this had first to be boiled for at least five minutes. The huge bamboo fires had to be kept alight 24 hours a day for this purpose.

We were awakened by the sound of Reveille while it was still dark, grabbed our mess dixies, and groped our way out through the thick mud to stand in a line, shiver, and wait for our gallant mess-orderlies to bring on our steak and eggs! The cooks had an unenviable task during the initial stages of the formation of Shimo Sonkurei camp, as they were compelled to cook for 2000 men on open fires in the pouring rain. On the evening of our second day it started to rain again, and continued for five days without stopping.

As anyone can realise, there were a hundred and one jobs to be done around the camp to make it anything like tenantable, but the Japanese ordered every fit man out to start work on the railway.

We were marched out across the road in front of the camp and into an old paddy field, which after the previous night's heavy rain was ankle-deep in water. Japanese engineers were detailed to take as many men as they needed for their allotted task for the day, and we were marched off to begin work on a railway which must go down in history as accounting for more casualties than many a battlefield.

Our section of the proposed line on the first day lay within a few hundred metres of the front gate of the camp, so fortunately we did not have far to march.

We gathered from the not very clear instructions of the Japanese engineer that we were to dig earth from either side of a straight line representing the course of the railway, and to carry the earth to build a sort of embankment. Other gangs began grubbing out the trees that lay in the path of the line. By lunch time, we had built an embankment about 150 m long.

We did not knock off till 9.30 pm, having worked for 14 hours. Just as we were moving off, in the direction of our camp, it started to rain again — and continued for five days on end.

Cholera had broken out at Shimo Sonkurei on a serious scale, and by May 23 we had lost nine men. By May 24 we could only muster 60 men from our company of 163 to go out to work. Other companies were in a similar predicament. On the same day, we received our second cholera inoculation, but not until after we had finished about 12 hours out on the line in the pouring rain.

Work on the railway was abandoned on May 24 owing to the futility of trying to build an embankment with the rain-soaked earth. Our efforts were diverted to repairing the road in front of the camp, which had become impassable due to the heavy rain.

I paired off with Sgt. 'Smoky' Doug Dawson, one of our unit from Manjimup in Western Australia; our job was to cart rocks and stones taken from the creek bed and dump them at various points along the road. Our equipment consisted of a primitive carrying idea called a *tunka*—an old rice bag through which two poles were strung, forming a makeshift stretcher.

Lumping one of these things all day was both arduous and monotonous, but by comparison with the job that some chaps fell for, ours was simple. They really 'copped the crow', standing all day waist-high in cold water, with the rain pouring down on their heads, and retrieving from the creek bed the rocks with which we were endeavouring to repair the road.

The creek-bed job was a fine way to catch pneumonia, and to it I attribute the death of at least one chap who was a member of our own unit. He was Norm Lane of Geelong, and a finer physical specimen it would have been hard to find anywhere. He was solid muscle and as strong as a lion, but he contracted pneumonia, from which he never really recovered, and died four months later—20 September 1943. Norm was normally about half my weight again, but a few days before he died of cardiac beri-beri and pneumonia, I carried him out to the latrines in my arms—he was at least two stone lighter than I was at the time!

We were very fortunate to have in camp at Shimo Sonkurei four fine medical officers. Headed by Major Bruce Hunt of Perth, they toiled day and night to curb the spread of the dreaded cholera. Despite their endeavours, by the end of the first week we had lost 40 men, and there were a further 97 suspects.

Due to the large number of men suffering from cholera, dysentery, beri-beri, tropical ulcers, pneumonia and so on, it was decided to reorganise the companies and their huts so that the sick could be congregated in several huts at one end of the camp. Major Hunt, our senior medical officer, and Major Anderson of the 2/30th Battalion repeatedly protested to the Japanese to allow those of us

Major Bruce Hunt AAMC, Senior Australian Medical Officer at Shimo Sonkurei Camp and Tambaya Hospital Camp, 1943.

who were still fit to remain in camp for a few days in order to put roofs on the huts, dig new latrines, build a cookhouse, dig drains, and repair the collapsed floors of nearly all the huts. For once the Japanese listened to reason, realising that unless a halt was called on the railway work there would not be one man capable of walking out of the front gate to work.

We were paraded for camp duties on the morning of 28 May 1943, and immediately volunteers were called for work up on 'Cholera Hill'. Fred McBean and I volunteered and were detailed off to report to the sergeant in charge of the cremation party—Sgt.

Burial at camp. Photograph: The Australian War Memorial

Crawford. The remains of the previous day's pyre were still smouldering when we arrived, and we immediately set about gathering sufficient bamboo and timber to build a huge bonfire.

During the morning we were brought four bodies to burn. We could not afford to lose the makeshift stretchers or the blankets covering the bodies, so it was necessary to walk in as close to the fire as possible and heave the bodies into the inferno. Of the time I spent on the Burma railway three or four days stand out in my memory, and the day I spent on the cremation party at Shimo Sonkurei is one of them.

Padre Polain of the 2/26th Battalion came up during the afternoon with eighteen bamboo urns about 450 mm × 75 mm to receive the ashes of the eighteen men who had been cremated during the past day or so.

The burial service, in spite of its simplicity, was very impressive, and I wondered if ever there was a stranger group took part in any soldier's burial. I remember at the time thinking of the very apt verse of 'The Burial of Sir John Moore', which I had learned from 'Pop' Rae as a pupil at Coburg State School:

Not a drum was heard
Not a funeral note
As the corpse to the ramparts we hurried
Not a soldier discharged his farewell shot
O'er the grave where our hero we buried.

We had no bugle, nor boots, nor shirts, nor shots to fire over the last resting place of eighteen of our cobbers. They were simply laid to rest in a very shallow grave in the thick jungle of Thailand, surrounded on four sides by tall bamboo and jungle vines.

Quite a few small crosses had been erected over the graves of those already buried, and together with the eighteen holes dug for the men buried that afternoon they almost covered the small area that had been cleared out of the jungle.

After the service, I welcomed the cigarette that Fred offered me, and sat on a log and enjoyed my first smoke for about nine months. Soon after lunch we cremated another two cholera victims and about 5 pm added another three, making a total of nine for the day. I was not sorry when Sgt. Crawford said that any more could wait until morning and we were allowed to go back to our lines.

The following morning, May 29, we were ordered out to work on the line again, and spent the day clearing a track through the jungle.

May 30 was declared another 'camp' day. During the morning, I helped Joc Dunn, a wee Scotsman from Western Australia, to remove the wool clip from several members of our unit. Joc, who was of course the experienced barber, laid bare the bald pates after I had clipped away the outer layer of hair with the scissors. I also asked Joc to remove the complete crop on my own head, as we all found hair a nuisance to keep clean, and it was far cooler without it.

During the day, Major Anderson the camp's senior officer, impressed on the men the futility of contemplating escape at this stage, as apart from the obvious improbability of contacting allied troops or reaching allied territory from our present position on the Burma–Thailand border, there was the question of the repercussions on the men remaining in the camp should the Japanese discover any one to have escaped. Furthermore, there were no medical supplies to spare for men who might attempt an escape, without which there was little likelihood of beating the inevitable jungle diseases that would accompany such a scheme. The only food available was uncooked rice, to which the men did not have access unless they had an accomplice in the cookhouse.

By 5 pm on May 30, we had lost another six men to cholera. Major Bruce Hunt likened our treatment not to that of POWs, but to that of slaves. On the same day, the text of the following letter was read to us on parade:

> Officer in Charge,
> Shimo Sonkurei Camp
> Thailand

The medical situation in this camp is extremely grave, and is becoming worse every hour. At the present moment, cholera is raging — there have been 37 deaths and there are over 90 patients in hospital. New cases are occurring at the rate of 25 or more daily.

Dysentery is still a very serious problem, and many men are so debilitated from prolonged dysentery or diarrhoea that it will be many weeks before they are fit for any form of work — meantime, their resistance to cholera or any other diseases is seriously impaired.

Malaria is rapidly increasing and we anticipate that within a week or two there will be hundreds of sufferers.

Taking the situation on a whole, it is our anticipation that within one month there will NOT be 250 men in this camp fit to do a day's work.

The reason for this situation is that the men in this camp have been subjected to treatment which is wrong for any civilised nation to inflict on its prisoners of war. In detail:

1 The men before leaving Changi were weakened by dysentery and deficiency diseases (beri-beri and pellagra) and were in no condition to withstand infectious diseases.

2 An assurance was given by the Imperial Japanese Army at Changi to the Commander AIF at Changi that food would be better here than in Changi, and the troops would not have to march from the train to their destination. Neither of these promises have been kept.

Relying on the second promise, many men totally unfit to march were included in the force — very many of these are now in hospital — some have died.

3 The hygiene of the camps on the road was appalling, and hundreds of men were successively infected by dysentery, by malaria, and finally by cholera (the present tragedy is the result).

4 The conditions of marching were extremely arduous, and in some cases unwarrantably cruel. Sick men were driven out on to the road night after night, in some cases with high fever, or active dysentery. As a result, when the men arrived here, they were completely exhausted.

5 After arrival, men were put in an unhygienic, badly situated camp, roofless, and with very bad latrine accommodation; all conditions ideal for the spread of diseases were present, and disease has, in consequence, rapidly spread — your own report that 53 positive results for cholera were found in about 500 apparently healthy men showed how rapidly and widely the spread took place.

6 No adequate rest was given to men, nor was any assistance given to requests for help. On the contrary, men were sent out to work and kept out of camp 12 to 13 hours a day in the pouring rain — conditions typical NOT of the honorable treatment of prisoners of war, but of slave labour.

At the present moment, (approximately) 37 men are dead of cholera; 95 men are in hospital with cholera; 250 men are in hospital with other diseases; 140 men are excused all duty on account of sickness, and many of these would be in hospital, if there were enough room or drugs or nurses.

One hundred and fifty are so weakened by illness that they are only fit for light duty.

One hundred and twenty men are being used (or have been used) in the care of the sick, and of these, 30 have already become so sick as to have been admitted to hospital. Thus about 800 men out of 2000 have become invalids or have been required to nurse the sick, within fourteen days of the arrival in this camp — and the number is likely to increase rapidly.

In view of the above facts, we demand:

1 That this document be forwarded to the representative of the International Red Cross in Bangkok or Rangoon.
2 That all work shall cease, NOT for three days, but indefinitely until the present cholera epidemic has been got fully under control. In this circumstance, we draw your attention to the promise given on the 27 May 1943 that all work would cease for three days. This promise was broken the day after it was given.
    The reasons for asking for all work to cease are:
    a To enable all necessary constructive work around the camp on latrines, roofing, and drainage to be done.
    b To enable hundreds of debilitated men to rest and recover their health.
    c To permit enough men being allotted to nursing work to give adequate treatment to the hundreds of sick, and rest to the present over-worked and exhausted nursing staff.
3 The supplies of adequate drugs, disinfectants, soap, lights, and other medical supplies.
4 The supply of blankets for the sick.
5 The supply of invalid foods, soups, and tea and sugar for the sick.
6 An improvement of the camp diet by extra vitamin containing food — for example — rice polishings, *towgay*, meat, oil and fats.
7 The supply of suppressive atebrin for the whole camp — the present small quinine dosage is quite inadequate and without effect.
8 The supply of water containers, especially 44-gallon drums to enable water to be used on a large scale, also similar containers for water boiling to make sterilisation possible.
9 The supply of a large number of tents (waterproof) for the cholera area, which is extending daily. At least 30 large tents are required, apart from what are now in the camp.
10 The supply of oil for dealing with mosquito breeding places in the camp — a visit from Capt. Wilson, malaria expert from HQ camp is urgently necessary to locate these.
11 The supply of protective clothing — white coats for nurses handling cholera.

12 As soon as the health of the camp has been improved, which
    may not be for several months, the evacuation of the area by
    troops and their subsequent treatment in a manner befitting
    the honorable Japanese nation, whose reputation must suffer
    gravely if the present conditions continue.

We demand that this document be brought before Lieut. Col.
Banno, and the senior Japanese medical officer for the area, and
also before Lieut. Col. Harris at the earliest possible moment—
preferably tonight.

> (Signed) Major Johnson
>   Major Hunt
>   Major Anderson

After the parade was dismissed I approached Major Anderson with
a view to obtaining a copy of the letter on the spot but although he
seemed agreeable his adjutant, Capt. Howell, considered this in-
advisable owing to the nature of the letter and the possibility of it
being discovered in my kit in a later Japanese inspection. It was not
until June 1944 that I obtained a copy from Major Hunt in
Singapore.

In spite of the warning given by Major Anderson, we learned on
the morning of May 31 that five or six men had 'shot through'
during the night. Among the party was a Warrant Officer who was
alleged to be still in the throes of an attack of malaria, and Doug
Weldon, the young chap from Barwon Heads, Victoria who had
the wireless parts in sealed pineapple tins at Ban Pong.

He claimed to have been employed by the large Far Eastern
shipping company, Jardine Matheson, at Shanghai, and had transferred to our unit, possibly from the Malay Volunteers, the day
before we left Changi. I believe he was 'planted' in our unit by
Intelligence for the sole purpose of attempting an escape to allied
territory. We never heard of Doug or the others again.

It was of course necessary to show these men as 'dead' on our
check parade figures but our own camp HQ must have shivered for
a few days when there was still a possibility of the party being
captured by the Japanese along the road to Burma. They must have
struck out for the west coast through the almost impenetrable
jungle. No doubt their bones still lie within a few miles of Shimo
Sonkurei, as no man could have gone very far under those conditions, and without equipment or supplies. As far as I know, no one
made a successful escape from the Burma Railway, though quite a
few attempts were made from various points along the line from
Moulmein on the west coast in Burma, to Ban Pong in Thailand.

On the morning of May 31 only 300 men were called to work
on the railway, but soon after 10 am they returned to camp, as the

A group, mainly British POWs, line-laying on the Burma railway, 1943.
Photograph: The Australian War Memorial

result of a demand made to Toyama by Major Hunt. The effect of such rare verbal victories by our officers over the Japanese, especially at such a critical stage, was inestimable. Judging from the camp reports of the very heated discussions that went on at the Japanese camp HQ it is a miracle that Major Hunt did not have his 'lolly lopped'!

Without detracting from the credit due to this man in a million, it must be said that in our camp we also had such wonderful doctors as Capts Lloyd Cahill, J. Taylor, and Frank Cahill, and Major Anderson and Capt. Howell of the 2/30th Battalion, who gave whole-hearted support to any advances to the Japanese for improvements in our camp conditions.

My shorthand diary records the following on 31 May 1943:

Worked all morning cutting bamboo poles. 53 deaths from cholera up to 12 o'clock midday. A very wet day. Percy Graham much improved after discharge from cholera hospital. Three 'yaks' being cooked for tea tonight (a great treat). Men still looking dirty, clothes in rags, unshaven, almost impossible to get water to wash. Boots worn out. No dry clothing. Men losing weight rapidly through lack of food. Now hopeful that consideration may be given to letter to Imperial Japanese Army as rumoured that about 800 cases of cholera among troops along the railway. No doubt that impossible for our troops to remain in this area as apparently the whole atmosphere infected with disease. Japanese issue of quinine tablets insufficient in strength to stop malaria, as plenty of cases being admitted to hospital each day.

I awoke in the morning of June 1 to find I had a badly swollen finger. This was as the result of the hair-cutting a few days previously, when I had raised a blister which had become infected. In ordinary circumstances it would not have mattered, but anyone on the Burma railway who had the slightest scratch would find that in a few days it had turned to a very painful tropical ulcer. I spent a miserable morning carting bamboo poles, then attended sick parade and was given 'no duties' for the day. I felt as though I was getting a dose of dengue fever, but no doubt it was the poison in my system which gave me that feeling.

We lost another seven men during the 24 hours to midday of June 1, bringing the total to 60. It was still raining, and the whole camp was a quagmire from one end to the other.

Fires were lit on the ground inside each of the huts in an endeavour to dry the few clothes of the working parties, and for the sick who had to make frequent visits day and night to the latrines in the pouring rain. In such a state as were dozens of our men at Shimo Sonkurei, it was possible to lose 500 g in weight with each motion, so that within a few days these men were just skin and bone.

The cholera cases were of course a far worse sight, and the speed with which they lost weight and their features changed was amazing. A cholera victim would usually have no prior warning of an attack, but within a few hours of wielding a pick or shovel along with the rest of us would be absolutely helpless, and hardly able to raise an arm through weakness. It was almost possible to see the flesh fading from their faces, the eyes would take on a glassy look and begin to sink back into their heads, giving them a ghost-like appearance. Their voices, whenever they found sufficient strength to speak, were almost inaudible.

Thirteen of the men from our unit copped cholera on F Force and only three of these, Horrie Ross, Fred Piera and Pearce Graham, recovered—but Pearce died later on after returning to Kamburei when the line was completed.

We lost another ten men on June 2, although Major Hunt, in his address the previous evening, had told us that the cholera position was improving. He did inform us, however, that the incidence of malaria was increasing and that more orderlies would be required, so I once again volunteered and was told to report to the fever ward next morning. However, next morning I was detailed by our company sergeant to assist in carrying the mess from the cook-house to the hospital wards. I did this job for a fortnight or so.

The rice was ladelled out into cane baskets, which we carted to the hospital wards at the other end of the camp. Considering that 1200 of the men in the camp were in hospital by June 4, our small gang of about ten men had no easy task, as apart from the usual three meals a day, we had rice water to cart each morning and afternoon. However, it was the best job I had on the railway, as our efforts were usually repaid with a good feed by the cookhouse sergeant.

Our unit was one of the few that had no officer on F Force, although there had been five when we left Changi. It therefore became the responsibility of our unit NCOs to protect our men. Fortunately the men from our unit supported one another throughout their captivity, and this was especially so on F Force. The Japanese would often put gangs of six men on contract work, perhaps digging a hole 9 m square by 1 m deep and carrying the earth to the railway embankment. When this happened we were able to 'carry' one or two who had recently been discharged from hospital, until they were strong enough to do a normal day's work.

I discovered that the mess carrying job was light enough to allow a sick man time to recuperate before being sent out on the road. When I was appointed NCO of this party on the third day, I was able to grab one of our own unit to fill vacancies whenever one of the ten mess orderlies was taken ill, as happened almost every day. Before long Allan Bassett, Junior Johnson, Norm Fox, Norm Lane, Billy Cook, and Des Dwarte from the 4th MT took their turns at this task.

On June 5 it stopped raining—we had not seen a glimpse of the sun for nearly a fortnight. Up to midday of June 5 there had been 84 deaths, including one poor chap in the convalescent ward who had choked while vomiting.

Padre Polain conducted our first church service on Sunday June 6 though few were able to summon the strength to rise from their sick-beds to attend. The fit members of the camp were, of course, working on the railway.

During the morning Major Hunt set out for the next camp, known as Sonkurei, occupied in the main by British troops. He returned in the afternoon with the news that the position there was even worse, and that they had lost 114 British and 6 Australians during the fortnight they had been there. Up till then, we had lost 90, but on the same day 26 men were discharged from the cholera hospital, and many of the other patients were feeling much better. However, of the 1900 men in the camp we could only muster 190 to work on the railway and of these perhaps 20 or 30 would be admitted to hospital on the next day. Practically every man in the camp was suffering from some form of internal or external disease, with the exception of course of the officers, who seemed almost immune.

Des Dwarte and I suffered an attack of 'trench feet', and found it impossible to stand in one spot for more than a few seconds as the tingling sensation was so constant. It was a severe form of tinea, brought about by standing in the creek half a dozen times a day washing cane baskets, and then walking around with wet feet.

I had been fortunate enough to pick up a pair of old boots on Cholera Hill, left behind by patients who had no need for them where they had gone. One boot was size nine, the other size six from which I cut the toe, but at least they were a left and right. They served me well for several months.

Owing to the appalling condition of the road, no truck could get within sight of our camp, and we were obliged to lump our own rations from the camp about 16 km further up the road. The first trip was made on June 8, and our chaps had to push and pull two-wheeled yak carts loaded with bags of rice along a road which was in parts axle-deep in mud. The operation was not a great success, according to Cpl. Lloyd Hoarse of our unit, who took part in the first ration party. It was soon decided to change over to packs and harversacks, in which every man had to carry 40 kg.

We learned after the return of the ration party that some of A Force were further north across the Burma border, and that among our own unit members there had only been four deaths since May of the previous year.

On June 10 we heard rumours that Mussolini was talking in terms of a possible defeat of the Axis powers. In our camp at Shimo Sonkurei was a Lieut. Wright of Ordnance, who had somehow or other smuggled radio parts along the track. Whether this particular news emanated from him I am not sure, as it was in our own interests not to know the source of any wireless news. However, it was gratifying to know that we could expect a bulletin from time to time. An immediate change would be wrought in the general atmosphere of the camp, and more particularly on the frame of mind of those that were knocking at death's door, when it was reported that the 'griff from our canary' (news from the secret radio) was good.

There was little encouragement for our men to live, when everyday was a nightmare from which there was little hope of awakening. In many cases, after prolonged struggles with sickness and debility, chaps would simply 'throw in the towel' and be dead within 48 hours.

We were slaves of the Samurai in every sense of the word.

Absolutely cut off from the outside world, we had not the slightest idea when or if we would ever see our homeland again. Many of the men were by now so deranged that they no longer cared and in the first few weeks there were at least two attempted suicides in our camp. Home was the foremost thought in the minds of the majority of us.

By June 12 we could only muster ten men in our company for work on the railway. The Japanese complained to our camp commander and threatened that our officers would have to make up the numbers. However, with the exception of those who went out in charge of the various gangs, the officers were soon found jobs as hut commanders and so on, and did not put their noses outside the front gate of the camp!

The Japanese increased the working party figures by 100 on Sunday June 13, and among the men who were to make up the number were those who had returned to camp about 1 am the previous night. We slaved in the pouring rain, barefooted and semi-naked, to the tune of never-ending *kurrahs* from the Japanese engineers and guards, followed by the inevitable crash of a bamboo stick on the bare back of some poor bloke who was too weak to lift his pick again. Men became afraid to stop digging for one second when the Japanese in charge was in the vicinity.

Owing to the state of the road, it was impossible for any heavy transports to get through without the assistance of an elephant to drag them out of bogs. It was therefore necessary for a party to march the 16 km to the ration camp every few days, thus reducing the number available for work on the railway.

On June 16, we persuaded the Japanese to allow us to work 'under our own steam', and contracted to complete the corduroying of several hundred metres of the worst stretch of road within two days. We finished the job, but not before we had all almost broken our backs carrying and laying the heavy logs.

It was first of all necessary to drain away the water that lay along the track, while a gang set to work chopping down trees in readiness for the log laying. The Japanese first loaned us an elephant to haul the very heavy logs to be used as a base, but on the second day they withdrew its services so we had to lump the logs on our own shoulders. Of course we had to do this anyway with the smaller logs, which must have weighed more than half a tonne each, but the base logs were much heavier, and of course required more men to carry them.

If his efforts were any indication that he was enjoying himself, Cpl. Ivor 'Sandy' Sanderson from Ararat in Victoria must have been having the time of his life. He took over the task of supervising the laying of every single log on our stretch of road, and the finished article was a perfect piece of workmanship. Cpl. Sanderson was responsible for the idea of building a corduroy road and had suggested it to Capt. Kearney as the only logical way of repairing the worst section satisfactorily. His action saved the whole camp from starving.

On the first day, we 'knocked off' at 8.30 pm and set off to march the 4 km back to camp. My feet were still very sore, almost red-raw with tinea, but we had to finish the job and were back at work early next morning.

Apart from one or two Japanese engineers who came to inspect our work, we were not worried by them during the two days we were working on the corduroy road. The men back at camp, of whom perhaps more than half were incapable of staggering more that a few hundred metres, had to be fed, and on their present ration would starve to death unless we made it possible for our ration trucks to get through. A few days later the rice ration was cut down to 35 kg for 1200 men in hospital—only for a few days, fortunately, but as I was by then a patient myself I experienced the pangs of hunger as never before.

We toiled all of the second day in an effort to complete our task before evening, but quite a few logs had still to be laid when darkness fell. The last of them was laid soon after 9 pm.

I had spent a very unpleasant afternoon with an obviously poisoned foot, and also felt the approach of an attack of fever, my first experience of many to follow. I hobbled back to camp through the mud as best I could, and was glad to lie down on the lumpy bamboo slats. I spent an uncomfortable night, and reported to our company commander at Reveille that I wished to go on sick parade. I can remember almost passing out during the five minutes or so that I had to stand in the rain outside the officers' hut waiting for him to appear.

After an examination later, I was admitted to hospital with malaria. The fever ward accommodated about 300 to 400 men, some of whom were already suffering their third attack of malaria since arriving in Thailand. The recurring type of malaria became an absolute menace to some men, who could tell almost to the day when to expect another attack. I spent a couple of very miserable days shivering and sweating under half a blanket, which was nonetheless more than some possessed.

The tucker was neither delectable nor plentiful, and for the first few days I found it difficult to get it past my throat, though there was always someone to help me out by eating it! Trying to reach the latrines in a fit of fever in the pitch dark brought its own problems, as without some means of support it was quite often a 'crash landing'.

I found I was as weak as a kitten, and became frightfully dizzy as soon as I had to stand erect. Before long I seemed to have lost another 10 kg, but this to me was no cause for worry as dozens of the bigger men had lost more than they now weighed! Unless you have seen it, it is hard to imagine what a man who normally tips the scales at about 90 kg looks like at around the 45 kg mark. Some of the poor wretches were walking skeletons, upon whose faces death was unmistakably written.

The Japanese quinine issue was doled out to us with monotonous regularity by the orderlies. There was a certain novelty about taking quinine for the first time, but after a few bouts of the 'bug' I began to loathe the stuff.

Our daily ration in hospital consisted of about 85 g (3 oz) of rice and a small cup of watery stew. However, the Japanese always maintained that if a man was sick he did not need or want to eat! Their ideas on the subject were not those of Major Hunt, who repeatedly stood over his patients and threatened to push the food down their throats if they were not willing to feed themselves. As he quite rightly explained, the food was the best we could expect from our hosts, and had to be eaten to survive.

While we were in hospital recovering, the remainder of the boys were toiling out on the railway line, and increasing reports came back each night of further bashings by the Japanese engineers and guards.

On June 24 I was feeling much better, and was able to stand up without immediately becoming dizzy. However, my feet were covered in small sores which quickly turned to ulcers. Paddling around in the mud was no cure for these painful skin diseases, and after a few days I went out with Ivor Sanderson to collect a couple of suitable pieces of jungle timber to make a pair of clogs, and thus began a full-time job for 'Sandy', because hundreds of men were without footwear of any kind.

On June 28 we lost our first man with typhus. Quite a few patients were in hospital with this disease, among whom was 'Butch' Barnier of Grafton, NSW. Butch was brought in off the road and lost consciousness soon after admission to hospital. He was placed on a makeshift stretcher, and lay there for three days without regaining consciousness. It was then discovered that for the whole three days he had been lying on an open kidney-shaped eating dixie, the sharp sides of which had eaten more than 25 mm into the flesh near the base of his spine. Gangrene had set in, and Butch soon had one of the largest and nastiest looking ulcers in the camp. He recovered from the typhus but was bedridden for a few months with the ulcer. Butch's case was another of the remarkable recoveries we witnessed in the absence of life-saving drugs. He was back on the line within three months.

About the same time as Butch Barnier went down with typhus, a chap was brought into our ward suffering from blackwater fever. Fortunately this complaint was a relatively rare one, as the victims are raving lunatics during the height of the fever. This poor chap was delirious, and kept everyone in the ward awake with his cries in the night and his muffled talk of suicide. He died within a few days.

On June 29 the medical officers made a special inspection of all sick men in hospital, with a view to removing the worst cases to a hospital camp about 80 km up the road at Tambaya in Burma, where they might have the opportunity to recover. The furphy later became fact, but not before many of those chosen to go had died. However, the mere idea of a shift from the present death-house gave the desperately ill a new interest and topic for speculation and discussion.

On July 3 the whole camp was awakened at 2 am and informed that one of the 'mad micks' (picks) loaned to the camp by the Japanese the previous day had not been returned, and that until it was found the camp's food ration would be stopped.

It is as well to mention here that quite a few of the men were 'going through' at night searching for any stray yaks along the track in order to supplement the daily ration. The animal would be slaughtered and brought back to camp in pieces, ready to be carved up for free distribution to their mates, or sale to those who could afford the price asked.

Quite a few yaks were driven down the road from Burma 'on the hoof' as a Japanese ration issue, but they were usually poor specimens. Several time those that were intended for the POWs cook-house (not the Japanese) were so close to dying they had to be held up to be killed.

Down at Nicki they had similar trouble with their yaks, but there the meat was used to thicken the stew for the camp as a whole, rather than that of a few individuals as was the case at Shimo Sonkurei.

It was suspected that the lost pick had been taken by one of the yak hunters. However, no-one claimed the distinction of having borrowed it, and the camp starved until 4 pm when it was discovered under one of the bays in the working party lines. It had obviously been placed there during the afternoon, as every inch of the camp had been searched earlier in the day.

Lieut. Cameron of the 2/30th Battalion, who was responsible for the care of the camp tools, had to answer to the Japanese for the pick, and remained tied up to a tree from 9.30 am till 3.30 pm!

Major Hunt was given permission to visit Nicki Camp on July 4, and returned in the evening with some encouraging news via the 'canary' (wireless) there. Good news was always very welcome, but it often brought with it a purge by the Japanese. Frequent bashings, and working days lasting till midnight were two ways of punishing their POWs for defeats suffered elsewhere.

On the three days following the news bulletin from Nicki, the boys returned from working on the line after 11 pm. Since no-one, including the cooks, knew when the men might return to camp, the workers, who had not had a bite to eat since the cold midday hash, would often have to stand around waiting for another half hour for their meal, in spite of their desire to lie down and sleep. On several occasions I returned to camp around the midnight hour and after drawing my ration, returned to sit on my bunk and eat it, but fell off to sleep to wake next morning to find that I had not touched a mouthful of it!

At this time, bashings along the line became more frequent and more severe, thus throwing an even greater strain on both victims of punishment and the other members of the party, who continued to wonder who would be next to be singled out. As compensation, however, we received our first ration issue by truck, and welcomed the arrival of onions, *towgay*, soya beans, and dried fish. Most of these were intended primarily for the sick, but the issue did not last for more than a few days, especially after the Japanese had taken their share.

On July 5, rumour had it that seven English officers had 'shot through' from Sonkurei, a few kilometres down the line, and the Japanese enforced a night picket comprised of men from our own convalescent ward to ensure there were no attempts to escape. We learned later that all the officers at the next camp were, as a result of the escape, confined to their quarters and refused food for five days.

The cholera epidemic was now almost under control, and the sufferers were commencing to regain some semblance of their former selves. However the Japanese camp commander insisted that some of the convalescents were now well enough to go out to work, and ordered that they be paraded to him on the parade ground next morning. Between 20 and 30 of the fittest convalescents were selected to parade, but of these several collapsed, and others had to be supported on the 150 m walk to be paraded before Lieut. Fukuda. He must have been shocked by the sight of these skeletons who could hardly stand, let alone walk, as he promptly forgot the idea!

However, the Japanese apparently decided that those few men that were fit for work would be worked into the ground, or at the least into hospital. On the night of 8 July 1943 the majority of the workers returned to camp at 2 am, thoroughly exhausted, though one unfortunate party did not return at all and we guessed the men must have either slept at Nicki or worked all night.

At this time, much to my disgust, I was languishing in hospital nursing a couple of slow-healing tropical ulcers on my legs and feet. Although I was anxious to get back to the working lines, if only because the rice ration was better, it would have been foolish to do so as I could not put a boot on either of my feet.

It was amazing the hours chaps spent discussing food, and the recipes they unearthed from books some had managed to carry in their packs. Many of the hospital patients wrote out recipes, pored over the beautiful ingredients and with surprisingly fertile imaginations endeavoured to appease their appetites on paper, but the idea of eating from a book did not appeal to me in the slightest, and only made me feel more hungry.

The hospital patients were shocked to hear on July 10 that the expected trip to Tambaya hospital had been cancelled indefinitely owing to the fact that railway camps further north in Burma had been bombed by our Air Force. According to the report Moulmein was being bombed fairly frequently. The high hopes of the men in hospital were dashed by this change of plans. However, a few days later we heard that 300 000 troops had landed in Sicily, preceded by a heavy bombing raid. This news of course boosted morale considerably, although everyone appreciated that successes on the European front could have little effect on our own position.

On the same day we heard that two chaps from our own unit on A Force, Vic Dahlgren and Len Walker, had been killed as a result of the air raids further up the line.

We also lost another good man at our camp to dysentery on July 15. Bill Bury, who was the luckless victim, had marched 304 km along with the rest of us just a few weeks after undergoing an operation at Changi for double hernia. Bill could have remained behind in hospital at Changi, but when the quota could not be made up from the men in our own company lines he fell for the bait of 'milk and honey' that was thrown to us by the Japanese, and decided to take the risk, and come along with us.

• • •

It was now two months since our arrival at Shimo Sonkurei. The 'canary' brought us our next news bulletin on July 19, informing us of the landing in Italy and of the fact that the invaders had advanced 140 km. It was also reported that we were shelling the French coast in preparation for a landing there, but this latter report may have been added for good measure.

I had by now been transferred to No. 2 Convalescent Ward, where I could do a few jobs around the camp. The very first day I went out to work, I had not gone two metres outside the gate when I copped a bashing from one of the Korean guards. Although I was not in charge of the small party of about ten men, I was wearing a shirt with a couple of stripes so the guard guessed I would suffice to show that we should have waited for his permission to move outside the gate. The NCO in charge of our party did not offer to make any explanation to the Korean, nor accept any responsibility for our actions, but allowed me to take the bashing. Naturally I did not 'dob' him in, but told him later what I thought of him.

It was rumoured that the proposed removal of the sick to a hospital camp was again likely, in fact it was added that the whole camp would be moving in the near future. We were instructed soon afterwards to discontinue all duties connected with extension of the present camp facilities.

We were all of the opinion that few camps along the line could be as poorly appointed as ours, but we learned after a brief visit by Major Hunt to Sonkurei that up to July 21 the British troops there had suffered 320 fatalities out of a total of 1400, whereas at our camp we had lost 123 out of 2000. It was also indicated that large batches of sick men there were compelled to work on the line — something we had so far been able to avoid. We were therefore grateful for small mercies, and thanked our lucky stars we had been born under the Southern Cross!

The most important job confronting the British troops at Sonkurei was the construction of a large wooden bridge over a wide fast-flowing river, beside which their camp was built. Several artists have depicted men working on these Burma railway bridges, but no artist could ever paint the agony and suffering that went to make up those deadly constructions. I know because I worked on several later on.

On July 23 I did my first full day's work for over a month and although still very weak, I lasted out the day, which started on the parade ground at 7 am and finished with a 4 km march back to camp at 8 pm. The work resulted in a couple of blisters on my hands, but I felt no other ill-effects.

Next day, we were out on the road on 'hammer and tap' — my initiation into this particular way of whiling away the hours. 'Hammer and tap' was performed by two men taking turns at swinging a sledge-hammer, or holding the long steel drill which is turned in a hole in a rock after each blow of the hammer. Sometimes when you are just learning the hammer misses the head of the drill and you hit your cobber's hand, but you soon learn not to miss!

It rained all bloody day that day; it was as cold as charity, and the bloke with whom I was paired was a bit of a 'drongo' so I was pretty miserable by the time I returned to camp. I finished the day by sitting up until 11 pm drying out my clothes for work the next morning.

The following few days found the camp in frantic reorganisation for the move to Tambaya hospital camp for some of the sick, and to other working camps for the remainder of us. At last there seemed to be something definite afoot.

During the last few days at Shimo Sonkurei I copped a beautiful dose of colic, due to eating either sour or inadequately cooked rice. I had more wind than a gale, and a breath resembling rotten eggs. I spent a few miserable days in the convalescent ward trying to dispose of the colic, after which I was out on the railway again.

As a farewell to Shimo Sonkurei I received as severe a bashing as I ever saw anyone else given. I was one of a small party that was given the job of building small bridges over a couple of culverts. The Japanese engineer, who had arrived at our camp during the past few days, was new to us, but we did not take very long to get acquainted.

I suppose he thought that as I was skinny and looked sick I would make a good 'king for a day'.

By the time we knocked off I was 'punch drunk', having been hit with almost everything on the job including an axe, shovel, a hammer, pliers, bits of cane — in fact, anything that was lying handy at the time. At one stage I almost 'did my block', but managed to control myself and twisted his arm up his back when he tried to come at me again. He knew I was 'fair dinkum' and after that incident seemed to ease up on me a little. The only other member of our small party that day that I can remember was S/Sgt 'Nugget' Plunkett of Ammo. Sub. Park, a South Australian unit, and he shared a few shovels with me when the Japanese handed them out!

Major Johnson warned us that during the forthcoming month the pressure would be on, but he hoped that we would be transferred back to Changi toward the end of August.

The Japanese made an unprecedented issue of soap and tobacco in those last days at Shimo Sonkurei. Most of the boys had their first wash with soap since leaving Changi, and after nightfall the huts were dotted with glowing pin-pricks as the men lay back and enjoyed their first smoke for several months.

It was not impossible to obtain tobacco or the more plentiful Burma cheroots from natives on the track. However, the price asked was usually prohibitive, as we had not received a cent from

The railway at Tam Krasaer, Thailand.

the Japanese for our work at this camp and very few of the men had any cash remaining from the proceeds of their black market activities at Ban Pong.

Even if we had been in a position to afford tobacco I am afraid we would have finished up chewing it, as paper supplies were almost unobtainable. Paybooks, for instance, were not worth a 'cracker' under our circumstances, and dozens of them went up in smoke. I always seemed to have a few spare sheets of paper and not being a smoker myself, was always ready to share with those who were down to their paybooks.

Many hymn books, and quite a few bibles and New Testaments made of invaluable rice paper ultimately became ash. I cannot say I approved of the idea altogether, but one padre reasoned that so long as the man read the page of the bible or New Testament before rolling his cigarette, he did not mind so much!

The first party of 300 sick and convalescents moved off to No. 3 camp (Kami Sonkurei) on the morning of July 28. They had a 15 km march ahead of them. After returning from work on Sunday August 1, our own company was instructed to pack its traps and prepare to move out for the same camp the following morning. I went to sleep wondering whether the conditions at Kami Sonkurei would be any better, now that we were leaving our Korean nemesis—Toyama—behind.

June

13/6/43. Sunday. Work party increased by 100, including men who stopped at midnight previous night.

Rumour that escapees had been captured by Japanese.

Rice ration cut down again.

Japanese supposed to have told Major Hunt and Camp Commandant that our own officers were responsible for all sickness and deaths in this camp.

Hundreds of Japanese soldiers moving up track all day long. Road impassable.

Almost called out for yak party during day. Yak stew in evening very nice. Gave Pearce Graham some of Japanese steak — very welcome.

Rained heavily.

Feeling fairly well myself and eating much better than anyone else in camp. Good appetite but feel very tired at times.

14/6/43. Yak party of 80 men to camp 10 miles away. Also large work party required on road.

Hospital mess orderly job cancelled, then reinstated.

Only 4 men required for kitchen.

Great confusion. Rice ration again cut down and hospital almost on starvation diet.

Japanese determined to send men out on road, sick or otherwise, and Major Hunt informed men that it would be necessary to repair the road to save ourselves from starvation as roads are still impassable by any transport at the moment.

Received letter and $4 from Oscar who has been working too hard and almost exhausted.

15/6/43. Worked on road carrying baskets of stones. Knocked off about 7 o'clock. Feet very swollen and sore.

16/6/43. First day's work under our own steam. No Japanese to worry us. Much better idea, but work very hard as under contract more or less to finish in two days. Carrying huge logs all day for corduroying of road. Really only possible way to repair these roads.

Knocked off at 8.30 feeling very tired and feet still very sore.

17/6/43. Out on same job again. Elephants taken away by Japanese making our work almost impossible as large logs very hard to carry out from in jungle. Hardest day's work I have done for a long time, especially as apparently got a touch of fever. Absolutely worn out when knocked off at 8.30 and walked 2½ miles back to camp with poisoned foot.

10

Birthday on the march

*M*onday 2 August 1943. My 25th birthday. We awoke to find it still raining, as it had been doing since early the previous day. It was of course still dark, and we scrambled out of bed to draw our mess, served by the light of the fire which as usual had been burning all night in the middle of the hut.

After stuffing our gear into our packs and haversacks, we moved outside to the company lines to await the final signal to muster with the others on the camp parade ground. Eventually, everyone was gathered together on the parade ground, where we were issued with our haversack ration of one pint of plain rice, which was to represent our midday meal.

Fifteen kilometres did not seem too far to march when we had covered twice that distance and more on several stretches of our long march from Ban Pong. We anticipated that we would reach Kami Sonkurei by midday, perhaps in time for a hot meal. Wishful thinking again!

We had been on the parade ground for some time awaiting word to move when we noticed quite a few stretcher cases being brought out of the huts. We guessed they too were being transferred to Kami Sonkurei, instead of to Tambaya hospital with the other sick who still remained. We were surprised to discover that most of the stretcher cases were the worst of the camp's dysentery sufferers, whom the Japanese refused to transport to Tambaya because their condition would cause too much inconvenience on the trip, and because in the opinion of the Japanese most of these patients were going to die anyway.

All of the stretcher cases had received an injection earlier in the morning to ease the pain of the trying journey we all knew was

Some of the cards the author received from Jack 'Long Tack' Thompson and Alf 'Snowy' Macklin during the years from 1942 to 1945.

ahead of them. We presumed that Japanese trucks would be arriving to transport the stretcher cases, as the roads were now usable if taken carefully.

I think our party totalled about 300, amongst whom were about 60 per cent fit, 20 per cent convalescent and the remainder hospital patients, quite a few of whom had been hospitalised for several months. In addition to our own minimal personal gear, there was more than the usual amount of cooking utensils, other containers, medical gear, and tent size Japanese-issue mosquito nets, as we had to carry enough for the earlier party of sick which had left on July 28.

One consolation was that the rain had eased up since Reveille. We were anxious to be on the move, as it was almost certain to start again before the day was over. We had already been waiting for more than an hour, when our company Commander shocked us by announcing that the stretcher cases were to be carried—*by the men*!

It is no exaggeration to state that these cases were, in the majority, more dead than alive. We could not believe that the Japanese expected us to carry them for 15 km. However, it was true, so I immediately sought out Lynn Martin, the only member of our own unit who was aboard a stretcher, and arranged for another five men to make up the six that could be spared for each stretcher.

The men to be carried lay lifeless on their stretchers, doped beyond caring of their whereabouts. Two of the men in fact showed so little interest in changing camps that it was decided not to go to the trouble of moving them, and they were picked up and taken back to the hospital from whence they had come. The poor fellows had not the strength to stand the strain of being carried from the hospital to the parade ground, and died before we had even moved out the front gate.

I had not expected any bells to be rung for my birthday, and started off up the road to our new camp, four of us carrying Lynn Martin while the other two lumped his personal gear. We had not gone more than 100 m before we were slipping and sliding all over the muddy track, with the stretcher biting into the bare bones of our shoulders and becoming heavier at every step we took.

I suppose I weighed about 50 kg (8 stone) at the time, and of the others in our stretcher party, Pearce Graham had just recovered from cholera, Des Dwarte had been in hospital with malaria, 'Darkie' Rickard of the 2/30th Battalion could carry on one shoulder only owing to an injury, and the other two whose names I have forgotten were in much the same condition as the rest of us.

We changed positions around the stretcher as frequently as possible to spell our aching shoulders. As we had only two reliefs, our spells from carrying the stretcher were brief. The stretchers were made of two bamboo poles and split cane, and before we had covered more than a few hundred metres many of them began to fall to pieces. The stretcher parties made whatever roadside repairs were possible from jungle creepers, or whatever they could find in their packs that might serve.

Our main worry was to keep our stretcher on as even a keel as possible and save Lynn being bumped about, but this was well-nigh impossible. The road was not very wide, and gouged with great deep wheel tracks filled with water. We trudged on as best we could, feeling our way with every step, expecting and often finding our feet slipping from beneath us and our patient close to being tipped into the mud. Fortunately, Lynn was in a state of coma until one particularly bad stretch of road, when we did eventually tip him out. He was so startled by the rude awakening that he did not slip back into his deep sleep and realised, too clearly perhaps, the task with which we were faced and his own position in the picture.

Before we reached Sonkurei camp, about the half-way mark on our march, we had all reached the point of absolute exhaustion. We rested at Sonkurei for about an hour to make repairs to our stretchers and to allow the stragglers to catch up.

Four of us on our stretcher finished the last two to three kilometres of the stretch to Kami Sonkurei without a spell, as the remaining two were unfortunately unable to carry on. At one stretch of the road shortly before Kami Sonkurei, more than a few found themselves spreadeagled in the mud as quickly as though they had slipped on ice. One young chap who had been following closely on our heels, suddenly slipped and fell, but had not the energy to rise again. He just lay there in the mud for a moment, then rose to his knees and with his arms raised to the sky started to sob out something about the Lord putting him out of misery. We went back and helped him to his feet and he staggered on with the rest of us.

As we came to within a half a kilometre of Kami Sonkurei we were overjoyed to see men coming out to meet us and relieve us of our burdens. No one can imagine how glad we were to see them, even though we had but a few hundred metres to go.

We marched through the gate at Kami Sonkurei about 7 pm on 2 August 1943, having covered 15 km in about ten hours, under conditions that are almost indescribable.

Those of us who had lumped the stretchers the full distance no doubt had the hardest task, and it was not very consoling to hear within a few days of our arrival that our efforts had been in vain, as many of the stretcher cases grew weaker and weaker, and all hope of saving their lives was gone. The buffeting they had received on the march had been too much for them to withstand, and quite a few had died within a week or two.

August

*4/7/43. Major Hunt back from Nicki camp. No further news of move.
Good news by wireless.*

*Billy Little very bad with tropical ulcers. Men arrived home from
work at 11.20 p.m.*

*Absolutely impossible to expect men to carry on under these
conditions with little food, hard work, and long hours.*

*5/7/43. Monday. Ration of onions, towgay, beans, fish arrived by
truck today.*

*News that seven Pommy officers and the colonel in charge of next
camp (Sonkurei) had gone through recently.*

Pickets posted at night time in our camp.

Men arrived home from work around 11 o'clock.

6/7/43. Still in hospital and feeling weak and very hungry.

Worked on paybooks in morning.

*Japanese camp commander instructed Major Hunt that he expected
cholera convalescents to now go out to work.*

*Twenty to thirty men paraded of which several collapsed and others
had to be supported.*

*Japanese getting very severe in their treatment of all men including
those on road who are being bashed about and made work terribly
long hours. Must be getting beaten somewhere.*

*7/7/43. Officers at next camp confined to their quarters and refused
any food for five days owing to officers 'going through'.*

Worked on paybooks all day.

Good 'doover' for tea in evening — very nice.

Burma move of hospital patients likely very soon.

Interviewed Major Hunt re job.

Men arrived in from work at ten minutes to twelve.

8/7/43. Thurs. Worked on paybooks all day.

*Still as weak as blazes no energy at all — quite understandable
considering food we are receiving — no nourishment in it at all. Also
pains around heart.*

9/7/43. Men arrived in from work at 2 o'clock in morning.

*One party not home at all — must have slept at Nicki or else
worked all night.*

*Ration situation improved at last. This morning hospital increased
to 12 oz, and workers in camp 18 oz and road workers 21 oz. Very
good breakfast hope it continues.*

One hundred and nineteen deaths in this camp up to date.

*10/7/43. Sat. Everywhere you go men talking about food and what
they are going to do when they return to civilian life.*

Thinking of home all day long and my own home when I get there.

Hope it will not be very long as I think we have suffered enough for any man during a whole lifetime.

Proposed move to Burma cancelled indefinitely owing to the fact that camps further north have been bombed by air force.

New Japanese guards posted at this camp and arms and ammunition moving up road all day so looks as though something doing up north.

Moulmein bombed fairly frequently according to reports.

Men in hospital very downhearted when told about trip being cancelled.

Spirits had been high as reports that tucker and conditions far better where they were going.

Hopeful that trip south back to Ban Pong will be made but very unlikely.

11/7/43. Itchy rash all over back, around crutch and legs. Very irritable.

Only 178 men available for road out of 1900.

Some cooks, and hygiene section etc. sent out to make up total of 200.

Fred McBean back from Moulmein.

12/7/43. Still in hospital. Ulcer healing up well. Still working on paybooks, but feeling weak and no energy at all.

News that troops landed in Sicily, 300 000 preceded by heavy bombing raid.

Four of our unit, including Vic Dahlgren and Cpl. Dennis killed in raid up north.

Very irritable cough at night time on chest — got couple of tablets.

13/7/43. Cholera and dysentery test by Japanese.

Fred McBean unable to buy anything or speak to anybody whilst on trip up north. Went up to lookout where Japanese on duty all time looking out to sea where islands are.

• • •

20/7/43. Still in convalescent depot. Doug Dawson out on road today. Bill Cook back in hospital with sore feet. Own feet improving daily.

Several photographs taken yesterday of men who had lost considerable weight since arriving here. Some men lost half hundred weight and everyones' bones sticking out all over.

Food bit better now but very few yaks killed.

21/7/43. First day's work since 17th June.

Very weak and cholic in stomach. However, finished day okay.

Bashed by bloody Japanese guard at gate. Very annoyed.

Major Hunt on parade in evening stating that hospital move on again also that no more camp duties as there may be a move shortly!

11

Kami Sonkurei camp

We found our new camp to be a pigsty compared with the comparatively well-drained camp at Shimo Sonkurei. The ground here was practically flat and received the seepage from the hill at the rear of the camp. It was ankle-deep in mud, and the first thought that struck all of us was how the occupants could have lived in such a place without doing something about cleaning it up, building drains and so on.

We spent our first day attending to the many camp jobs and carrying bamboo for the cookhouse fires. During the afternoon, a few hundred British troops arrived. Having already spent a few days with them on the march from Ban Pong, and being aware of their high rate of mortality along the line, I had to agree that their arrival was not a very welcome addition to our already over-crowded quarters.

Predictably, they arrived with very few cooking utensils, which meant that those our chaps had carried all the way from Ban Pong would have to be shared with them. Somehow, the British were unable to exhibit the initiative or adaptability of our chaps, and often failed to show the extra spirit that was needed to pull through when they were seriously ill.

One consoling feature of our new camp was that there appeared to be an abundance of rice, and rumour had it that prior to our arrival here the few hundred men had lived very well, and the death rate had not been high. We hoped that the camp's good record would continue, but fate ruled otherwise.

On August 4 we rose at 6.30 am. In fact, it was about two hours earlier as the Japanese always set their watches to Tokyo time. Mess was served by the light of the bamboo fire inside the hut, and we sat on the edge of the bays and ate our breakfast.

After the company roll-call we were marched down a narrow alley-way, past the Japanese guard-house and onto the road for a Japanese check parade (*tenko*). Each morning and evening the men would march past the guard-house in file, giving the *Kashira Migi* or *Kashira Hidari* (Eyes Right or Left).

About a kilometre of the line near the camp was already partly finished, but the day after our arrival the Japanese engineers decided that the present path of the track was not suitable, and changed its direction! We were marched back to a spot within 100 m of the camp, where work had already been started on the usual embankment.

It was pouring with rain, and our job was the usual one of carting earth in a *tunka* to the embankment. Being water-sodden, the soil was sticky and as heavy as lead; to add to our difficulties, the embankment could only be approached by the narrow paths left between sections where the earth had already been dug to a depth of 1 m. At times we had to trudge through mud up to our knees, often finding it impossible to withdraw our feet and overbalancing with the weight of the *tunka*, thus adding a bit more Thailand mud to our blackened bodies.

We had become accustomed to misfortune in our time as POWs, but even the most stoical paled at the news that awaited us when we returned to camp on the evening of August 6. Upon leaving Shimo Sonkurei we thought to have quit forever our former camp and guard commanders, Fukuda and Toyama, but we learned that they had trailed us to our new camp!

My diary for the next few days simply records that we were working on the line, very tiring and long hours. Breakfast was eaten in the dark, as was the evening meal. On several occasions soon after arrival at Kami Sonkurei I almost missed out on tucker because I usually insisted on walking to the creek and scrubbing off the mud from head to toe. I could then eat my rice on my bunk, fall back and be sound asleep within a few minutes.

For six days, I had been working in my bare feet from sun-up until late into the night, with the Japanese engineers driving us on with increasing severity in an effort to complete the task allotted. On the sixth day I found that I could barely put my left foot to the ground, as I had contracted an ulcer between my big toe and the next one. The mud oozed in and out of my toes, increasing the agony with each step I took.

I reported to Capt. Jutner, our medical officer from South Australia, who ordered me into hospital. There was little in the way of medical supplies for treating ulcers and it was up to the individual to bathe them with water as hot as it was possible to stand, as often as water could be obtained. However, I must admit my ulcer was nothing compared to some with which other chaps were cursed.

Everyone knows how painful it is to touch a sore or an open cut, but it is impossible to imagine the pain some chaps suffered when their ulcers were being scraped with a hard silver spoon! One young chap I knew came to two of his cobbers one morning and, with the tears almost rolling from his eyes at the thought of having to go through a similar experience to that of the previous day, asked if they would mind coming out of the hut to hold him up while Major Stevens scraped the ulcers on his legs.

I forced myself out to witness a few of these parades, of which the ulcer cases were absolutely terrified. Their screams rent the air as the silver spoon penetrated into the tender flesh to remove the thick green slime. Several fainted, but the majority just ground their teeth and hoped it would soon be finished. Major Stevens' task of administering the scraping was an unenviable one, but he would sit there on an old log outside the hut each morning calmly scraping away as though the patients were so much wood.

Cholera broke out at Kami Sonkurei on 10 August 1943 and we lost four men during the first night. We were immediately inoculated once again against the disease we had all come to dread.

Contrary to the report that August was usually the worst month of the monsoons, the weather was comparatively good; as a result the camp gradually began to dry out and our spirits were lifted a little. The food situation was not improving, however, and our water supply was inadequate in spite of the earlier heavy rains. The creek was placed 'out of bounds', when cholera began to claim further victims.

Friday August 13 brought with it more bad news when I was informed that Lynn Martin, whom we had carried from Shimo Sonkurei, had died suddenly. Lynn's bunk was in a bay directly opposite my own, and on the previous day I had paid him a visit to find him reading from his Bible. He told me he was feeling very much better, though his frail frame hardly confirmed his optimism. We had sat in silence as the distant strains of the Last Post and Reveille reached us from the hill at the rear of the camp, where four Australians were being buried.

Although it was agony to put too much weight on my ulcerated foot, I made the effort to walk the 500 m up the steep hill to the cemetery, as I could not find any other members of our unit fit enough to attend.

The service, which was held in the late afternoon, was attended by Col. Kappe, the senior Australian officer on F Force; Capt. 'Skipper' Allen of the 8th Division AASC; Sgt. Pat Byrne, who had transferred to our unit from General Base Depot; and a bugler from the 2/29th Battalion. Our Roman Catholic padre, Padre Walsh, conducted the burial service and a simple wooden cross was erected over Lynn's shallow grave.

That day, two parties were sent to the camp 7 km up the road, only to return empty-handed. Prospects for the next few days were not improved when in the evening 500 native workers arrived from down the line, where it was rumored they were dying at the rate of fifteen a day from cholera and smallpox.

On August 15 all the men at Kami Sonkurei were again given the glass-rod treatment; 25 men were found to be cholera carriers, amongst whom was Capt. Jutner, one of our medical officers. The carriers were immediately isolated in an area on the other side of the road fronting our camp, and although they were not affected physically by their condition they were treated more or less as hospital patients, and were not available to work on the railway.

Toyama continued to make his unwelcome presence felt about the camp, especially when the 'canary' began to whistle good news of allied victories either in the Pacific or in Europe. About this time we heard that Italy had 'thrown in the sponge'.

Toyama threatened to reduce hospital rations by half unless a certain number of men were turned out of hospital immediately to carry bamboo for the Japanese cookhouse. Since this drastic action would have jeopardised the health of all patients, the required number was found among the convalescents. At that time we were sleeping fourteen men to a bay 3.5 m by 4 m, though shortly afterwards we had to cram sixteen into the same space, which made it practically impossible for anyone to turn over or rest on his back.

It was reported that F Force had already lost 2000 of the 7000 men who had arrived less than three months previously. At Sonkurei, about 8 kms down the road, the death rate was already over 40 per cent, though before the line was completed they had lost 1200 of their original 1600.

Cholera continued to claim many victims, and a further 59 carriers were detected on August 17 after another glass rod test. The Japanese were very frightened of this disease, and many of them were afraid even to enter the wards where cholera patients were billeted.

The camp was one morning surprised to see several hundred more 'Tamils' arriving, presumably to occupy our camp, though goodness knew where they were to be billeted. The Japanese ordered that the huts of the working party lines be vacated immediately to accommodate them. When the workers returned that night their gear and bedding had been thrown out on the ground in a heap; and in the dark it was like looking for a needle in a haystack, and few were successful in recovering their own belongings.

The influx of natives necessitated the erection of a second level of bays in our huts, but the top level collapsed on the very first night and the occupants of the upper storey had to sit up for the rest of the night. The supports were strengthened the following day and apart from an occasional mishap, they were quite a success.

I was still in hospital at the time, though my ulcer was slowly getting better, and I was looking forward to being discharged in the very near future. This was even more desirable as the tucker in the working lines was more plentiful than in hospital, where we were absolutely starving. I think that our ration was then the lightest we ever experienced as prisoners, and although I hate to have to admit it, on several occasions I went down to visit a cobber of mine in the working lines to see if he could spare some of his food!

On Sunday morning, August 22, the men turned out for working parties at the usual time only to be informed that another glass rod was to be administered during the morning. The air was thick with abuse of the Japanese nation and Toyama in particular. It was no doubt his instruction that the information had been withheld until the workers had turned out in the mud and slush, when they could have been spending a precious hour or two catching up on lost sleep. Twenty-five further cholera carriers were found in the workers' lines, of which 23 were British troops. My pal, Des Dwarte, from whom I had obtained some tucker a few days previously, was admitted to hospital with an attack of malaria, from which he suffered regularly. I spent the day trying to make him as comfortable as possible, but without much success, as one's bones usually protruded so much that lying in the one position became quite painful.

Our hospital was such in name only, and existed for the men to remain in camp long enough to allow them to recover enough strength to go to work again.

The dysentery and ulcer wards were particularly nauseating. The bamboo slats and the ground in the centre of the huts were often fouled with excreta until an orderly or a patient could manage to clean it up. Most of the dysentery cases were incapable of making the trip to the latrines. They had to rely on the orderlies hurrying over with a piece of open bamboo, or use one of the few small cane chairs and bamboo pans that were available. Quite often the orderlies were too busy, or the chairs were occupied—and dysentery, like time and tide, waits for no man.

The walking skeletons in the dysentery ward were a terrible sight. Their skin seemed to take on an unnatural darkish-brown colour after a few days of uncontrollable bowel discharge. Victims were rendered helpless in a very short time, and often men were unable to give warning of a spasm, or to rise from their beds to help themselves, so that the horrible mess was spread all around them, and more especially on their one and only blanket, for there was no replacement while it was cleaned and washed. When coming back to camp at night, the air was so polluted that we could smell the camp 200 metres down the road.

Nevertheless, the struggle between life and death continued. Our camp doctors, Major Stevens and Capt. Jutner, with the assistance of the willing and capable orderlies, fought every fight to the last atom of strength, preferring to forget that the battle was in lots of cases hopeless and the result a foregone conclusion. Capt. Taylor, the 2/30th Battalion Medical Officer, reiterating Major Hunt's remarks, urged his patients not to give up, and through such urging and care, more men than was likely clung on until they could return to Singapore, and eventually home to Australia.

The task of our doctors was an unenviable one, and their impotence in the absence of suitable drugs must have caused them considerable distress. Capt. Jutner, whose attitude towards his patients was criticised by many, was in my opinion one of the most confident and capable doctors we had on the railway. It was just that his air of assurance was interpreted by many as a lack of interest, when his examination of a patient seemed cursory or when he seemed distracted during a lengthy detailing of symptoms. Capt. Jutner invariably exhibited an attitude of complete indifference towards the Japanese, and it is a pity a few more of our officers did not try to emulate him!

By August 28, my ulcer had improved to such an extent that I asked to be discharged from hospital. However, I was not too happy about the prospect of working bare-footed and I approached one of our own unit NCOs, whom I knew to be unlikely to work again, and asked for a loan of his boots for a few days until my feet had hardened up once again. He refused! I had stolen tucker from the Japanese cook-house for this man, I had often obtained a bucketful of scarce hot water and bathed him when he was too ill and weak to do so himself. He knew that he would not wear boots again on the railway.

He died several months later after we moved back down the line, but during that time I spoke to him again only once. My attitude toward him was dictated by a feeling of disappointment in someone who, under the worst conditions in the world, had betrayed the hand of friendship.

• • •

I recommenced work on the line on August 29. Toyama ordered a kit inspection outside the huts as soon as we returned to camp. I hid my diary and other papers on my person, and proceeded to lay out my gear on the ground with the other boys. Toyama decided to examine the kit of our company personally!

He came across my paybook, a few papers, and some photographs belonging to Lynn Martin which I had intended handing to his wife upon my return to Australia. I told him they belonged to a 'dead man'. You would have thought he had received an electric shock. He flung them away all over the place, as though they were so much rubbish to be carrying. I retrieved the photos, and replaced them in my pack.

• • •

On August 31 we completed our section of the railway embankments to the point where the men from Sonkurei camp were working. We also received our first pay, my enormous portion being $1.50.

The Japanese followed the annoying practice of handing over the total pay in notes of large and useless denominations. Where were we expected to change large notes into smaller ones, 300 km from nowhere? One pay-day, I was given the name of six workers, including my own, and told to distribute the pay among them. Apart from the difficulty this presented of changing the notes, one chap whom I did not recognise maintained quite adamantly that *his* name was on my list. I insisted that he was not, and read the names out to him. He declared that he was in fact so-an-so from the 2/30th Battalion but this chap certainly looked nothing like the one I knew, who wore a long luxurious beard! I finally realised that the transformation in appearance resulted from a long overdue shave. Shaving in the dark was a tricky task, and razors were at a premium, so many men sported 'flowing' beards for long periods.

The embankments now completed, our next task was to erect wooden bridges from timber hewn out of the surrounding jungle. Trees in the gullies lying in the path of the line were chopped down and trimmed for use as piles or bearers. Holes were dug in which to stand the piles, and a temporary structure erected high above the ground in order to drive home the long piles once they were finally in position.

The Japanese decided to tackle the highest and longest bridge first, and to do this we had to obtain logs varying in length from 16 m down to about 4 m. Some of the largest logs were at least half a metre in diameter and were damned heavy.

We found that whenever a job required a little more technical knowledge than usual, the Japanese engineers would begin to panic, and bash our boys for no reason at all. This was especially the case in building railway bridges where we had heavy logs to carry on our shoulders.

One of the bridges built along the Burma railway. Photograph: The Australian War Memorial.

Twenty or thirty men, sometimes more, sometimes less, would be spread along the log without any prior grading of their heights, so that the weight of the logs when lifted was unevenly balanced on the shoulders of the taller men.

Of course, the difference in heights was always quickly remedied by the taller ones stooping to allow everyone to share the weight equally, but the unnatural position did not make it any easier for carrying.

We soon evolved an idea to simplify the lifting, and to avoid irregularity caused by some lifting before others. Someone would usually give the call 'One–two–lift' and slowly the log would rise — chest high, pause, then on to the shoulders. Then would start the back-breaking struggle to lug the log to its required position. Usually our path was over rough ground, and through thick scrub. When we crossed a narrow dip in the path, the log would leave the shoulders of some carriers, thus throwing the whole weight moment-arily on the shoulders of the others.

It was hard enough for us to carry these logs, but the job was rendered even more difficult by the Japanese engineers assaulting us with sticks as we bore them along, urging us to more speed. Many a man was injured for life straining to lift beyond his strength whilst heavy blows rained down on his back.

The bridge building offered comparatively easy tasks to those who understood something about carpentering, or were cheeky enough to say they did, but most of us were compelled to join the gangs of log carriers and pile-drivers.

The pile-driving was technically a simple affair, though rendered difficult by the fact that the logs were 16 m to 20 m in length. The apparatus for driving the piles was known to us as a 'monkey', and consisted of a huge square iron weight suspended over the top of the pile. Above this had been erected two pulleys, through which very stout ropes were threaded and pulled out to the ground below. At the end of each heavy rope, fifteen or twenty thinner ones were joined and spread out fan-wise. Our job was to pull on these ropes at the given signal of 'Lift–one–two', and up would come the heavy iron weight till it had reached a certain height, then down would crash the weight on top of the pile. The sudden jerk on the ropes as we let go almost pulled one's stomach out, but we had no time to think about our worries before down would come the call 'Prepare to lift', and so it went on all day.

One compensating feature of our days on the pile-driving was the beautiful, sunny days we experienced, really the first we had seen since our job began on the line. It was a change to wash sweat from one's body in the cold running water of the nearby creeks, instead of a layer of mud. The sudden change was as welcome as 'the flowers that bloom in the spring'. One of the last possessions I threw away on the march was my book of Gilbert & Sullivan operas!

By the end of the seventh day on pile-driving I had just about 'had it'. My night's slumbers were accompanied by the yelling of the sergeant high up on the scaffolding — 'One–two–lift' — and no doubt most of the others on the same job were similarly affected.

When we returned to camp in the evening of September 5, we learned that four English officer escapees and a Malay had been captured and were being held in a small hut near the Korean guards' quarters, across the creek from our huts.

It was rumoured that they were to be executed, but according to reports they all looked so sick after their ordeal in the thick jungle, that they probably could not have cared less. They had been at large since early in July, during which time they had lost five of their party. Even with the most up-to-date medical equipment, food supplies and jungle fighting tools, I doubt that picked men in the fittest condition could have attained success in reaching the west coast through the impenetrable jungle of Thailand and Burma. The four British officers were among the ten who escaped from Sonkurei camp, which was under the control of Colonel F. J. Dillon.

The following day, September 6, we were thrilled to receive an issue of ten Japanese cigarettes. This was the first of quite a few we received during the next few months, and proved a source of revenue to non-smokers. The more important topic of the day was a 'furphy' that supplies from a canteen at Sonkurei would be available to those of us who had the necessary funds. Some few days later a party marched to Sonkurei to collect the goods that had been purchased by the boys. Naturally, endless discussion and fore-thought went into the spending of each man's few treasured dollars. It was as if each of us was spending his lifelong savings on one investment, and worrying about whether it would return as much as hoped for. Furrowed brows weighed whether a tin of fish at $2 would represent better value than condensed milk at $3, or whether *gula malacca* (sugar) was better than pig fat. Apart from these four items, there was little else from which to choose, but after our usual diet these few items seemed to offer the variety of a fully stocked grocery store.

My seventh day on pile-driving represented my last for a little while, as I 'blacked out' in the afternoon while pulling on the 'monkey' and was admitted to hospital once again with a dose of fever. I rested in the shade of an old log that was used as a 'back log' by the 'billy' boilers, and with a few other *bioki mai* (sick men) waited until the Japanese guard allowed us to return to camp with the mess-containers that had been brought out at lunch time.

I went on sick parade in the evening, feeling very sorry for myself, and after having my temperature taken—minus a thermo-meter—I was ordered into hospital. As usual, I could not look at rice for a few days after starting the four-hourly doses of quinine.

I was able to sit up and take a little nourishment by about the fifth day, and felt even better when it was reliably reported that Italy had capitulated. Whether this was true or false does not matter, *we* were told she had.

On the night of September 14 the boys did not finish until 2 am, and were back out on the line by 6 am. I returned to the worker's hut that day and spent the afternoon carrying bamboo poles for the kitchen fires. In the evening we received an issue of tooth powder (more like powdered charcoal dyed pink) and a few Burma cheroots, which were accepted with enthusiasm. A party from No. 5 camp, further north over the Burma border, passed our camp that day on their trek down the line and told our boys that the rails had already been laid past their camp.

September 16 saw me once again up with the larks at 5.30 am and out on the line. In order to get me used to the work gradually, the first day's work was finished so that we could reach camp by 9.45 pm! And it had rained all flaming day.

On September 18, Reveille was as usual at 5.30 am. Des Dwarte and I had arranged to collect each other's mess on alternate days to save both of us trudging around outside in the dark in the rain and mud and slush of mess parade. We ate our gruel, fell in for work parade and made our way past the Japanese guardhouse onto the road fronting the camp. There we sat for nearly 2½ hours in the rain waiting for the Japanese engineers, who had lain in their beds till 7.30 am. Reveille had been changed without any prior notification to our own HQ.

However, in spite of a bad start the day ended well, as it was the one for which we had waited for nine nightmarish long months. It marked the date, 18th September 1943, on which the first train passed Kami Sonkurei camp.

I often wonder if the driver of that first diesel train gave a thought to the number of men who had given their lives so that Nippon might build a railroad to Burma. Japan had succeeded where Britain had failed, ironically enough at the cost of British lives which the latter had not been prepared to risk when she abandoned the scheme back in 1907 or thereabouts.

We had returned to camp in the evening by the time the line-laying crew commenced placing railway sleepers in position, just outside our camp. Our boys were not thinking of the value of the railway to Japan when some gave a rousing cheer as they heard the diesel train pass our camp. The rest of us simply heaved a sigh of relief that our 'hell on earth' might now be nearing an end, and that soon we might return to a less inhospitable climate. Sixteen hundred men of F Force already lay buried along the line, and many more were to die before we quit the Burma railway.

Sunday September 19 represented the first holiday for all members of the Kami Sonkurei camp, and sleeping in until 7.30 am was like a dream come true. The Nips, however, decided to grasp the opportunity to repair some of their tools, and being among those who had spent only a few days on the railway during the past week I was included in the party to report to the Japanese guardhouse.

It rained solidly all day, but as our task of putting wire handles on the Japanese jungle knives was performed in the guardhouse, it was not so unpleasant. At lunch time, we drew our mess from the Japanese *squeshi-bar* (cookhouse) and partook of a thick yak stew.

Within 10 m of where we were working, a Korean guard was mounted on the small hut in which the English officer escapees had been kept since their arrival. I often wondered what became of those men, and whether they were executed as we expected they would be. It was more than 40 years before I happened upon a book, *Toward the Setting Sun*, written by James Bradley, one of the English escapees, who had somehow managed to record details of their six weeks' ordeal in the Thailand and Burma jungles, their eventual capture by the Japanese, and final transfer to Outram Road Gaol in Singapore.

Upon reading the chapters covering the escapees' capture, and their return to the railway camps, I realised that James Bradley had been unaware of his exact whereabouts along the railway, as he referred several times to his incarceration at Thanbyuzayat camp in Burma when they were actually imprisoned in the small hut at our camp, Kami Sonkurei in Thailand.

At least, after 40 years, I was able to clear up the mystery, and it was good to know that these brave men had somehow survived to tell their story. After checking dates and shorthand diary details carefully, I was able to write to Mr Bradley in England and let him know my own slight contact with him and his fellow escapees at Kami Sonkurei camp, and clear up the misconception regarding the actual camp in which he had been imprisoned.

The evening of September 19 gave us a further opportunity to enjoy a 'smoko', as ten cigarettes were issued to each man.

Work on the railway being at an end, we were next put to work in a quarry right beside our camp. Hammers, weighing anything from 900 g to 3.5 kg were issued to the men, and about 600 of us took up positions to crush the huge boulders which had already been blasted out of the side of the quarry.

Most of us knew little about breaking stones, or the ease with which injuries could be caused by the razor-edged chips of rock flying through the air. We soon discovered that it was not how hard you hit, but where you hit, that counted—but not before many an unlucky worker had been sprayed with flying chips of rock, each one a perfect starting point for a tropical ulcer.

Naturally there was a certain amount of risk in working among 600 men, and often more, in a quarry about 140 m long. There was only the one face to the quarry, and this rose to a height of 10 or 15 m in places, and fell away gradually almost to ground level.

The first two days' work in the quarry at Kami Sonkurei were, like lots of others, very wet and miserable, but of course we were in a much happier frame of mind now that the railway was finished. However, we were continually being reminded of the seriousness of our situation by the ever increasing death-roll, which rose sharply on September 20, when 12 Englishmen and 4 Australians were added to the list 'Died Thailand 1943'.

Norm Lane from Geelong, a member of our own unit of whom I have written earlier, was among the four unfortunate Australians. He died from pneumonia and the dreaded cardiac beri-beri. Beri-beri had been known for many years as a disease caused by malnutrition and normally marked by paralysis of the extremities and severe emaciation or swelling of the body, but we were led to believe that cardiac beri-beri was unknown to the medical profession until our experiences on the Burma railway. The loss of men with the physique and stamina of Norm brought home to us only too clearly how lucky some of us had been to escape cholera, dysentery, beri-beri, regular bouts of malaria, large tropical ulcers etc., any two of which if contracted conjointly usually resulted in a long spell in hospital, with little prospect of recovery.

Norm Lane had finally become victim to cardiac beri-beri, but his condition had been weakened by the severe bout of pneumonia he had suffered earlier at Shimo Sonkurei, where he had been forced to work in the cold creek bed in pouring rain for days on end.

For many years after we returned to Australia my wife and family regularly drove the 80 km from Melbourne to Geelong, and often wondered whether there was any connection between Norm Lane and the Geelong suburb called Norlane. Research revealed that a small group had approached Norm's widow soon after the war to seek permission to use the name Norlane for the new suburb.

Due to the bad state of the roads, our camp stopped receiving rations for a few days towards the end of September. No doubt our officers asked the Japanese why it was not possible for our rations to be brought down by train, now that the line was completed!

Owing to the late hour at which we usually returned to camp, it was generally not possible to visit our sick cobbers in hospital at night, so many of us made it a practice to slip through the wards on our way out to work in the mornings. Quite often we learned to our sorrow that one of our mates had died overnight. Such was the case on the morning of September 27, when Billy Cook and I ran into one of the huts yelling out for Pat Byrne, who had recently been admitted with cardiac beri-beri.

We found him with a blanket pulled up over his head, and were shocked to learn that he had died a short while before our arrival. Pat, who had transferred to our unit with Sgt. 'Oscar' Wiles and Des Dwarte, had been dogged by bad luck ever since we arrived at Shimo Sonkurei, where he had, very early, contracted dysentery. He had plodded on, working on the line whenever he could gain sufficient strength to be discharged from hospital, but in the end his strength had given out.

Des Dwarte and I applied for permission to be left in camp on September 29 so that we could attend Pat's burial service. Had the line not been completed I doubt that we would have had the audacity to ask. Padre Walsh performed the service. He told me later that 192 men lay buried in the small cemetery overlooking our camp. With the exception of about fifteen, all had died since our arrival in the first days of August, an average of three a day.

Now that the railway was finished, there were constant speculations about when we could hope to move back to Singapore. No one could have hoped and prayed as hard as we did, but nothing eventuated for several months, during which time death's dark shadow hovered continually over our camp.

Captain Taylor MC (AAMC) and Major Johnson, both of the 2/30th Battalion, paid us a visit from Sonkurei on September 27 and reported that suspected smallpox had broken out among the natives there. This put the 'kybosh' on any ideas we had of moving back to Kamburei and Singapore, and the Japanese declared that we must remain in case the disease had spread to Kami Sonkurei camp as well. We were inoculated for smallpox in the evening.

The work was now comparatively easy, most of the original Japanese engineers having gone from our camp, and the replacements being not as anxious to maintain our customary 'speedo' programme. Even 'Bull', a Japanese engineer who had remained, allowed us three hours for lunch one day when we were adjusting sleeper heights and picking ballast on the line.

The trips to Sonkurei to collect canteen goods became a regular procedure now, and on one of these I marched along with Padre Walsh. I have already spoken of Padre Walsh's constant care for the men of F Force, and the solace he provided in their darkest hours. Padre Marsden of H Force was another who earned the undying respect and gratitude of the men on the Burma railway. On the line, in the hospitals, a man was a man irrespective of his religious beliefs so far as Padre Marsden was concerned. I know of an occasion when he came to the cholera ward late one evening to perform the last rites for two men of his faith, who were not expected to live through till morning.

My pal, Malcolm Stevenson of Moorabin, Victoria who had probably never been inside a Roman Catholic church, lay dying between these two chaps. When asked if he would like the Last Rites performed, Steve replied that he was not a Roman Catholic, but that mattered not to the Padre, who saw only a man who was very soon to be swallowed up by death. Fate took a turn, however, and Steve was found to be still alive next morning, much to the amazement of everyone. Steve lived through to tell himself the story of Padre Marsden's kindness.

Another member of F Force who helped to maintain the strength and morale of the sickest men of our own unit was a cook, employed at Shimo Sonkurei in the Japanese cookhouse. He was 'Tich' Redding, and although he may have been disliked by a few, I always gave him credit for doing a good job on the line at a time when our tucker was shortest, and the Japanese had more than enough to satisfy their own needs.

Tich used always to reserve some of the Japanese evening meal for the boys in hospital, but of course it was a risky matter to keep this from the prying eyes of the guards and smuggle it to our lines across the creek from the Japanese quarters. After dark I would go down to our creek ostensibly for the purpose of having a bath, with a dixie and perhaps a tin concealed beneath my towel, awaiting an opportunity when no-one was about to attract Tich's attention and take over the 'handout'.

The Japanese became suspicious when their egg supply became exhausted rather too quickly, and they guessed their AIF cooks were responsible for the shortage—which was of course quite correct, as the eggs were being sold at about $5 a piece.

Tich did not pass any eggs to me, but the discovery meant that we had to be far more careful, and quite often the handout had to be abandoned when guards were spotted near the cookhouse or on our side of the creek. The Japanese threatened to deal with anyone who was caught, but the fact that they had good food to spare in their kitchen whilst our sick men were starving to death persuaded those of us who were running the gauntlet to persist.

One evening, with a dixie full of thick stew and another over-flowing with an invaluable supply of salt, I made my way up the path to the top of the creek's steep embankment, and just as I was about to turn the corner of the bamboo fence separating our camp from the native quarters, I ran slap-bang into a Korean guard.

The dixie of stew was obvious, but I had thrown my towel over the salt to hide it from the envious eyes of our own men. I pretended not to understand when he asked what was underneath the towel, and told him I was taking the dixie for the *bioki mai* (sick men) in the hospital.

Whether this statement struck a remote spot of pity in his heart I shall never know, but he did not as much as lay a hand on me. I held my breath while he threw a few unmistakable oaths at me in his own language, then just glared at me for a second or two and told me to go. I walked back to our lines as if in a daze, wondering how on earth I had managed to escape after being caught red-handed.

The following day our kits were inspected once again by the Japanese, but by this time I had of course distributed the salt to the most deserving cases of our own unit members. Among the Koreans inspecting our kits was the guard I had encountered the previous night but few of my pals would believe that this particular guard, with his reputation for brutal assaults, had allowed me to go free with tucker stolen from the Japanese kitchen.

A few days later Tich Redding was bashed by Toyama complaining that the mess dixie in which his food had been served was too dirty. Toyama was as unpopular among his fellow guards as he was with the POWs. The Korean guards feared and despised him. It is fitting that Toyama was among the first war criminals to be convicted and hanged at Changi gaol, Singapore.

Although the railway had been completed for almost a month, it was not until October 16 that we saw the first steam train pass our camp. Small diesel trucks containing sleepers, etc. had passed our camp daily to continue laying the line further south, but now the line was declared safe for the much heavier steam engines.

We were still working in the quarries to crush rock for ballast on the line, and at intervals this would be loaded onto railway trucks and carted away. There were actually two quarries at Kami Sonkurei, one right beside the camp, and the other several kilo-metres north toward the Burma border. A day out at the far quarry always presented a major problem for the 'billy boilers' because matches were non-existent, and it was usually necessary to carry hot coals from our camp cookhouse fires in the bottom of a bucket.

On October 20 Des Dwarte and I were due for the billy boilers job at the far quarry. As we marched along the railway line we wondered how in the hell we were going to light our fire, as no party had been out there for a day or two and there would be no embers remaining from earlier fires. Fortunately we came across an old Thai squatting over a miserable fire beside the railway line about half a mile from camp, so I went over and selected the best of the three sticks on his fire. You would have thought I had stolen all his worldly wealth, as he burst forth with a tirade of abuse which fortunately I could not understand. Des and I felt deeply grateful to him anyhow, as we would have been most unpopular had we not been able to produce a cup of 'char' for the boys when they knocked off for their 'smoko'.

• • •

On October 21 we were granted a *yesame* (rest). I took the opportunity of visiting Gerry Rosenberg, who was very ill with pneumonia. Gerry nearly always worked with Des and me, and we had found him to be a terrific mate and a good worker. He was on the dangerously ill list and had been in isolation for about a week, but I knew there was no question of his throwing in the sponge, like one of his own close friends had done a few months previously when he contracted dysentery. Gerry told me later that he had done all he could to persuade this young lad to battle on reminding him that we must soon see the end of our days as prisoners, and that he had everything in life to live for. However, he was determined to die, which he did a few days later.

One would imagine the easing of our workload with the completion of the railway might have seen a lessening of the death rate. In fact, the reverse was the case, as with the passing of each week our bodies were becoming more vulnerable to disease, for which drugs had long since been exhausted.

We lost fifteen men in the 24 hours between the mornings of October 22 and 23, and by the end of the same month the total death roll for our camp had reached the alarming figure of 348, nearly all of whom had died in the small space of three months.

The monsoonal rains had by this time abated; in fact our camp was suffering from a lack of water, as the creek upon which we relied for supplies was getting alarmingly low. The spot where we were permitted to wash was not made any cleaner by the presence of a half dozen ducks, which insisted on paddling in the shallow and already muddy stream. They were, of course, the property of the Korean guards, but many an envious eye pictured them in our cooking pots.

Our rations were confined to the usual rice and yak stew, and the lack of vitamins commenced to affect more and more of the men with beri-beri. Once the swelling rose above the thighs there was usually little hope, especially when the genitals reached unimaginable proportions. Laurie Pope, an old schoolmate of mine from Coburg, contracted this form of beri-beri. He died before we were moved back down the line.

Although we had no way of knowing whether the famous horse race was actually being held, we reckoned that Tuesday 2 November 1943 would be Cup Day in Melbourne. So far as we were concerned, it was just another day nearer home, and even that was rendered somewhat doubtful when during the morning it was reported that a case of cholera had been found among the patients. The report proved false, but the doctors were taking no chances and we received another bamboo rod test and a cholera inoculation the following day as a precaution.

For the inoculation we were given a *yesame* so I took the opportunity of visiting all members of our unit who were then in hospital.

Among them was one of our unit members from Western Australia who, although not as seriously ill as some other hospital patients, refused to feed himself or to assist in his own recovery. I went to see him in the morning and evening, and after having unsuccessfully tried to persuade him to feed himself, finished up feeding him with a spoon.

I am afraid I was inclined to agree with his nearby bedmates that he was a hopeless case, and was not surprised when the following day an entry was made in his paybook: 'Died Kami Sonkurei November 4, cardiac beri-beri'.

In contrast to this man's despair was the case of a patient in the ulcer ward, whose leg was amputated at the thigh by Captains Jutner and Taylor on November 3. The operation was performed with a limited number of instruments, in the open air under a large mosquito net. Even with the best of attention and food, an amputation of this nature would have been traumatic, but this bloke realised that the job had been done to save his life. He is probably one of the many 'limbless soldiers' of the Burma railway who are walking around Australia today.

Another of our fellows who put up a long fight was Jock Dunn, also from our WX section. Jock had, like many others, been weakened early by the ravages of dysentery, but had intermittently been a member of the road-gang when not in hospital. He was made of the right stuff, and was always included in the 'handouts' from the Japanese cookhouse, as I felt it would pay dividends in the long run. I was therefore alarmed to hear from his mate George Lumby that Jock had lapsed into a coma on the night of November 12, and much unhappier to find on our return from work the following evening that he had died.

Jock's death brought the total in our camp to approximately 420, and although only a handful of this number had died before our transfer from Shimo Sonkurei early in August, the first fortnight of November had claimed 70.

The whole camp was suffering from scabies on the backside, frontside, legs and arms, and whenever possible we tried to relieve them with sulphur baths. Everyone's gear was alive with grey hard-backed body lice, and one subconsciously cracked them with the thumb-nail as they bit during the night. They usually sought refuge in the folds or joins in our clothing and would often make sleep impossible.

I know that I used to be very annoyed at having my night's sleep disturbed, as the short time in bed was all too precious. However, even a mild case of beri-beri made an uninterrupted night's sleep an impossibility, and the embers of the hut fires revealed a never-ending flow of men stumbling dazedly to the urinals to relieve their bursting bladders, quite often not making the distance.

Some of the workers tried using large bamboo containers at night and although they were not exactly hygienic, and were unpopular with the majority of us, they were even more so when accidentally spilled by those sleeping in the top bays.

Our move, we were informed, had been definitely set for November 17, so Padre Walsh held a memorial service before we departed. I can still see that motley group of dirty, unshaven survivors, squatting on the ground or leaning against the huge log outside our hut; their bony bodies showing the effects of the diseases they had all suffered. Few had footwear of any kind, and the rags they wore were all they possessed. Many remembrance services have been held since that day in November 1943, but none as simple or as moving. We sang 'Abide With Me' and remembered our mates who were now buried in the shallow graves in the cemetery nearby. We would not, could not, forget.

Later in the day, mine being one of very few 'cut throat' razors in camp, I became a rather reluctant barber for about an hour. The last customer, Eric 'Junior' Johnson of our unit, wanted it shaved off, not pulled out, and departed half way through my performance.

My blade razor usually had a finely sharpened edge, as there were those with plenty of time as well as the expertise and equipment to sharpen them. Safety razors were a more difficult proposition, and some men would spend hours sitting patiently turning the safety blade around inside a Marmite jar in an effort to retain a cutting edge.

12

The road back

November 17 was the day for which our boys had waited and prayed ever since they first set foot in Thailand. The heavy rain which had fallen during the night could not dampen the spirits of those men who had been chosen to move off with the first train-load, and they sat around all morning chatting excitedly like a crowd of schoolgirls.

At 12.30 pm the 300 lucky members of our camp were called to parade and then marched out on the road. No sooner did they get there than they were brought back into camp again. The parade was dismissed, and the men returned to their lines to squat on their now very depleted packs and await a further call. It was not until 6.30 pm that we again made our way out onto the road fronting the camp. As luck would have it, it immediately began to pour. In a few minutes we were soaked to the skin, and our gear equally as wet. We sought refuge under the collapsing floor of the nearest Thai/Burmese workers' hut, but the driving rain soon sought us out there. We sat huddled, awaiting the arrival of our heaven-sent conveyance, which did not materialise for several hours, by which time we had almost given up hope.

When it did arrive we were told that 50 men only could be taken, and the remainder of us were ordered to move up independently to the huts on the hill at the far end of our camp. It was by this time about 11 pm, and all of us were glad to 'bed down' for the night and see what the dawn would bring forth.

The next day too we remained all day on the hill camp with a diet of plain rice and ginger water to keep us contented. Soon after Reveille on November 18 we were ordered to march down to Sonkurei camp, about 8 km away.

We learned that two of our men at Sonkurei were very close to death. Both of them were suffering from beri-beri. Of the two, Bill Gass of South Australia was undoubtedly the weaker and our boys were resigned to the fact that he would be among the dead men calculated to each railway sleeper. His was one of the amazing recoveries, however, as he fought the disease until he was strong enough to make the 300 km train journey back to Kamburei, and eventual return to Changi. Like many prisoners of war, he died a few years after his return to Australia.

The waters of the river at Sonkurei, over which the men there had built a large bridge, looked inviting and we cooled off there during the afternoon and rinsed out the few rags we called our clothes. Few had money to spend, especially at the exorbitant price of $1 the Thais were asking for one banana.

We stayed the night at Sonkurei and moved off for Nicki Camp, a distance of about 15 km, early next morning. Everyone moved under his own steam, and the men were straggled out for several miles along the track. Of course, the fittest of the marchers were soon well out in front and were rewarded for their fleetness of foot by being ordered into the waiting railway trucks when they reached Nicki camp. There were only two trucks available, so the first 50 were the lucky ones. As the remainder of us arrived, we were shown to tents and huts within a few hundred metres of the railway line, and instructed not to move too far away from the area.

We found some of the 2/29th Battalion boys here, and for the first time encountered Dutch and Javanese troops. We learned later on that the Japanese had taken away a well-known identity from Kami Sonkurei and shot him beside his own grave. He was a big Irishman we all knew as Paddy, a man of huge proportions, tattooed chest and arms, and with a voice and laugh that left no doubt that he did not give a damn whether he was on a railway in Burma or a tram in Belfast. Paddy was violently ill at Nicki and the Japanese suspected that he was suffering from smallpox. Had this proved true, and spread to the troops generally, their plans for clearing F Force from the area would have gone awry. They therefore took the easy way out and shot him!

We filled in the day at Nicki swimming in the deep, wide, fast-flowing river and getting a few hours sleep before the slow tiring journey we knew lay ahead. Night fell without signs of us leaving so we retired to our beds, only to be awakened at about 11 pm with orders to fall in immediately and move up to the railway line. We might just as well have stayed where we were, as we had to sleep in and out of the trucks beside the line until next morning, when we drew some plain rice for breakfast and a ration for lunch.

It was on the morning of November 21 that I had my first ride on
the railway—our train moved off at about 7 am. The first stage of
our journey back to Kamburei lay over very hilly country, and it
was really quite beautiful, though difficult to appreciate from our
crowded positions in the trucks.

We were crammed 30 or more to a truck, and our only seats were
the contents of our depleted packs. 'By goom Moom, your boom
gets noom' after 50 km or so, and the scabies adorning the posteriors
of 99.9 per cent of the travellers did not help.

It was a very slow journey, and we made our first stop in a thick
jungle area at 1 am. We had been travelling for 18 hours, and were
well and truly ready for a sleep. The boys soon had the area lit up
with their own little fires and prepared for a few hours 'shut eye'.
However no sooner had we lain down, that we were ordered back
into the trucks and moved on down to what we knew earlier as
'Regimental camp', arriving there at 4 am.

We stayed there all day, and ate our first eggs and fish for six
months or so, which made everyone feel much happier. We left just
on dusk, after having been ordered in and out of the trucks for
numerous *tenkos*, and then travelled all night. The train was held up
for quite a while when one of the trucks was derailed, but we felt
ourselves fortunate when we learned a few days later that some of
the trains were derailed as many as seven times during the 300 km
trip. We arrived at Kamburei at about 7 pm on November 23, and
then marched the 2 km to the camp. Now that we were back in
civilisation we were all anxious to participate in the delicacies which
had been denied us during the past eight months. Eggs, fish, and
bananas were plentiful and cheap, and daybreak saw the men
scrambling through the scrub to reach the Thais who were offering
their wares—away from the prying eyes of the Japanese guards.

It was at Kamburei in May that Fred McBean had almost lost his
pack, but it was my own that a Thai chose to lift the day after we
returned there. Fortunately, I was still fit enough to give chase, and
I succeeded in recovering it. I do not suppose there was 'two bob's'
worth of stuff in the whole pack, but to me it represented all my
worldly wealth and I was not anxious to part with it.

Parties from up north continued to arrive during the next few
days, and we enquired from each of news of our mates who had
been sent to the hospital camp at Tambaya, on the other side of the
Burma border. Some we learned had not recovered, but I was
pleased to hear that among others Doug Dawson, Peter Bellairs,
'Oscar' Wiles, Horrie Ross and Bill Little were on their way back
from Tambaya.

Peter Bellairs was still a boy when I had left Australia, but in 1943 he had already gone through the Malayan campaign as a member of the 2/26th Infantry Battalion, and survived several years as a POW. I had had absolutely no idea that he was in Malaya until a few days after our arrival at Changi, when I heard someone enquiring the whereabouts of Jim Boyle and was horrified to discover that the voice was young Peter's. He had been the youngest member of the office staff where I had worked before leaving the company to join the army in 1940—and I had imagined that he would still be working there. Peter would have been back in Australia before his 21st birthday came around!

• • •

The full report of events at Tambaya Hospital Camp is best left to someone who was actually there. Sufficient here to mention a few details. It was situated on the main Burma–Thailand line, approximately 150 km from Moulmein on the west coast. It was under the command of Major Bruce Hunt, our 'lifesaver' from Shimo Sonkurei Camp.

The patients were removed to Tambaya from down the line in motor trucks and although among the worst cases were many dysentery sufferers, the Japanese insisted that none of these be included. As many as 22 men died on the trip from the working camps to Tambaya, a distance of around 100 km. Although stops were made at various staging camps along the line, the Japanese insisted that all bodies, dead or alive, be delivered to Tambaya in order to keep their 'books' balanced.

The total number of men transferred successfully to Tambaya in August was in the vicinity of 1900, but by November there had been 681 deaths! Of these deaths, 61 per cent were British, and 39 per cent Australian. For some reason, the Australians had proved themselves more hardy. Perhaps it was the heat or perhaps it was a question of stamina. Undoubtedly, it was also the mental attitude of the Australians, and their ability to adapt to changed circumstances, that played a large part in the recovery of many.

The camp rations would arrive at intermittent intervals by train trucks, but they were little better or larger in quantity than those we received in spite of the fact that supplies were more accessible.

Three weeks after arrival of the sick at Tambaya corporal punishment was introduced by our officers to maintain discipline, and to preserve the 'protection' which had been afforded this hospital camp. Surprising as it may seem, looting of mates' kits prior to or following their deaths was rife right along the line. Most of us had little of value by the time we were sent to the Burma railway, but saleable articles often found their way into the hands of detestable thieves when kits were not carefully watched.

On one such occasion, three weeks after the establishment of Tambaya camp, an Englishman stole a watch from one of his mates. He was paraded, and awarded four lashes. A sentence of twelve strokes was imposed on another chap later for stealing a towel and shirt. Soon after, another patient who was suffering from dysentery, beri-beri and ulcers, and who was naturally enough classified as 'confined to bed' was found by the Japanese guards about a kilometre away from the camp trading with the Burmese. In order to prevent other hospital patients from jeopardising the safety and health of the troops by incurring punishment from the Japanese (in the form of ration cuts, etc.) this chap was awarded twenty strokes of the lash. The following day the same chap 'shot through' altogether only to be captured 48 hours later by the Japanese.

As was to be expected, there was much controversy over this form of punishment when F Force eventually returned to Changi, but I am firmly of the opinion that such a course of action was justified, and the officers who often administered the punishment were only carrying out their duty in order to safeguard the interests of the remainder of the camp. It was all very well for officers at Changi to criticise action taken by Major Hunt, but no one apart from those who helped to build the Burma railway was in any position to pass judgement. Compared to the conditions on the railway, Changi was a palace.

Maintenance of a sufficient supply of water at Tambaya hospital camp was also a difficult problem, especially during the latter stages of 1943 after the rainy season had passed. The camp kitchen was forced to move its position three times and finally, when water had to be carried almost a kilometre, it was shifted down to the river.

There were dozens of leg amputations at Tambaya, and I believe three only of these men eventually returned to Australia. Of these, one was Lionel Crooks of our own unit, and another was an original member of the Changi Concert Party, whose lusty baritone voice had lost none of its fine qualities when we heard him back at Changi gaol in 1944–45.

The doctors often had to borrow an ordinary hand-saw from the Japanese with which to perform the amputations. Most of the amputations were the legacy of tropical ulcers which had eaten away all the flesh from the bones. Naturally, every endeavour was made to save a leg or arm with the limited supply of medications and by constantly bathing the ulcers with hot water, but when these treatments failed amputation was the only alternative.

By the end of November, when preparations were being made to move back to Kamburei, it was found that 250 of the patients could not possibly have endured the long, tiring train journey. It was decided to leave them behind in the care of a selected number of hospital orderlies, in the hope that some at least might recover sufficiently to be moved at a later date.

If proof were required of the severity of the illnesses of the Tambaya hospital patients, it was clearly evident when 46 of them died on the train journey back to Kamburei. Even after arrival there, a further 186 died in the first few months in spite of the far better food and hospital conditions.

The story of Tambaya Hospital camp is one of a constant battle against death, and those of our men who returned from that camp will readily admit that it was their good fortune that a man such as Major Bruce Hunt was in charge of it. He was largely responsible for its establishment, its maintenance, and the final recovery of many men who would assuredly have died had they remained at the various working camps, from which they had been transferred. He should surely have been honoured by the Australian and British governments for his dedication and service to fellow prisoners of war.

An inscription on the Kohima Memorial in a remote, mountainous area of Burma speaks for all those who died:

When you go home
Tell them of us and say
For your tomorrow
We gave our today.

November

1/11/43. Working in quarry today not very much doing. Very lazy day.

2/11/43. Melbourne Cup Day. On water boiling. Cholera scare. Fortunately reported after lunch that another form of dysentery. Also news that move within a week.

Received six eggs and a few doovers from 'Tich'. Had for supper.

3/11/43. Holiday today.

Received 'dung punch' and cholera inoculation.

Visited all patients in hospital.

Frank Croxford not too well and refusing to eat in spite of fact receiving best tucker in camp. Amputation at thigh by Capt. Jutner and Capt. Taylor in tent in open under mosquito net.

Creek almost dry.

Engineers moved away today.

Fed Frank with spoon morning and evening meals.

4/11/43. Working on road today. Did very little work and only a few engineers left at this camp. Knocked off about 5 o'clock.

Frank Croxford died this afternoon. Cardiac beri-beri.

5/11/43. Working in quarry loading trucks.

News that moving in about five days.

Rained nearly all day. Fairly cold day.

5/11/43. Working in quarry stacking stone. Had cold shivers in morning and fever in afternoon. Feeling pretty crook went on sick parade in evening and blood slide taken.

Japanese building new huts in this camp.

Look like moving any day now as Japanese taking away stores and stew containers.

Issue of 4 pigs to our kitchen.

7/11/43. Carrying bamboo for cremation centre in morning. Still with fever and feeling weak.

2/29th Battalion arrived No. 2 camp today.

Medical supplies issued to hospital by Japanese.

Frank Croxford buried today.

Nearly everyone in camp troubled with itch, scabies and sores all over body. Now being treated with sulphur baths.

8/11/43. Working on railway on fettling work. Bloody bastard of a Japanese to work for, but three hours for dinner.

9/11/43. Same type of work again today.

No news of canteen yet.

Report from Burma that 600 dead in last two months. Jack Nolan, Bob Allen and Dick Simpson dead in Burma (Tambaya Hospital). Lionel Crooks had leg amputated.

13

Kanchanaburi camp 1943

K amburei (abbreviation of Kanchanaburi) was much the same as it had been earlier in the year, with tents scattered here and there in the clearings among the scrub. It could never at any time have been a good camp, as the nearest river was over 2 km away, and water had to be carted in the few trucks made available by the Japanese. Uncleanliness would not have been tolerated in normal circumstances, but the long march to the river was only undertaken by those with sufficient reserves of energy, and a conscience which told them they must sweeten their filthy bodies for the lice and bugs which were still part of our night-life!

Had I not been among the group that went to the river on one such occasion, I might have continued to partake of all the good things that were available at Kamburei, and have continued to replace some of the weight lost up on the line.

However, with the few meagre dollars at my disposal I bought cake from a Thai stall near the river. I fear it had not been baked under the strict supervision of the health authorities. Within a few days, I was suffering from my severest attack of dysentery, and at the same time I seemed to be vomiting everything I had eaten for the past six months.

The condition continued for days, and try as I might I could not get any food, even delicacies such as bananas, eggs or sweet coffee, past my throat. Although I attended sick parade, the MO was rather unwilling to accept the fact that I was sick. It was the first time I had been really crook, and I did not need any MO to confirm the fact. I was kicking myself that I had chosen the only place in two years where tucker was plentiful to put myself on 'no diet'.

At least I had the consolation of knowing that my own mates in the tent realised I was sick, and they assisted me as much as possible. One of these worded his disapproval to the RAP staff after one of my many nocturnal excursions to the bore-hole. He was sitting by a camp-fire outside our tent with a few of his cobbers when I rather dazedly made my way past them, and he asked if he could give me a hand. I proudly declined the offer, but he was just in time to catch me before I collapsed to the ground.

I was out like a light, and he called an orderly from the RAP to come and see me. It was then near midnight, so it was decided to defer closer examination till the following morning. The same orderly returned soon after sick parade the next day and with little hesitation diagnosed me as having a dose of yellow jaundice!

I had by this time lost almost 13 kg, and as I could not have been more than about 50 kg when I arrived at Kamburei, any old tune could have been played on my bones. Apparently I was not a very happy sight, as the reports that went back to my two cobbers, Jack Thompson and Alf Macklin, at Changi when F Force returned there were that they were hardly likely to see me again as my condition was pretty low.

Perhaps my condition was low, but my spirits were not, as I had not gone through the experiences of the previous six months or so just to succumb when we were back in a land of milk and honey. I had not given a moment's thought to the possibility that I might not come out of Thailand, but was cursing my fate at being stricken when there were available so many good things that had been denied us for so long.

Among the men at Kamburei were the remnants of H Force, which had been sent up from Singapore a few months after the departure of F Force. Twenty four men from our unit had been sent away on H Force, of which 30 per cent died before the end of November. The remainder who had now returned to Kamburei included Mal Stevenson, Lieut Bob Hughes, Max Banks, Ab Birthisel and 'Shorty' Stidwill, all of whom were good mates of mine. They were warned to 'stand by' for an early return to Singapore, and apparently it was decided to include me with the first train load. Orders came through that we were to leave Kamburei on the morning of December 10, so my cobbers packed my bags and helped me over to the parade ground, where I just sat and waited like the rest of our party.

The announcement that I, and three or four others, would be travelling to the railway siding in an ambulance was as good a piece of news as I could expect. However, it was a long while afterwards that it actually arrived, by which time the remainder of the troops had marched the 2 km to the siding and entrained.

When we arrived at the railway siding I discovered that the truck to which I had been detailed was at the rear end of the train about 150 m down the track. Somehow, I managed to get my pack on my back, and set off with the feeling that I *had* to make it. It was probably the slowest 150 m I had ever covered, but I did not finish it alone. As soon as my own unit pals, Horrie Ross and Bill Little, sighted me they came running to give me a hand. I was lifted and pulled into the truck, and made as comfortable as possible on the floor at the rear. There I sat befogged and wondering when the long tiring journey back to Singapore would begin.

I had arrived in Thailand feeling as fit as the fittest, but now I was leaving with just the barest fraction of luck to be getting away at all.

November

14/11/43. Out to work today. Loading trucks very easy day knocked off about 4 o'clock.

Canteen stuff cancelled.

Scarcity of cigarettes and tobacco.

Slept outside for first time. Moonlight night and heavy dew.

Bought pack of Red Bull cigarettes $1.

Another row over in Japanese cookhouse.

15/11/43. Holiday today. Work stopped altogether. Attended memorial service.

16/11/43. Organised in train and truck groups. Not sure of time of departure.

Canteen party down to No. 2 camp.

Shaved a lot of chaps during day.

Rained very heavily during evening.

17/11/43. Waited all day for train to arrive. First train load of three hundred taken out on road at about 12 o'clock and then immediately brought back.

Paraded again at 6.30 on road. Started to pour rain at 9 o'clock and everybody sopping wet. Only 50 men left on train, remainder sent back to camp.

19/11/43. Moved to No. 2 Camp where meals just as bad. Had swim in river during afternoon.

20/11/43. Marched down to Nicki and first train load of fifty men sent away in morning as soon as arrived at Nicki. Remainder put in tents and huts.

Dutch and Javanese camp at Nicki also 2/29th.

Went to bed but awakened at about 11 o'clock and moved up to station where slept until morning.

Drew plain rice for breakfast and also midday meal.

Moved off at about 7 o'clock.

21/11/43. Very slow journey over very hilly country.

Meals very bad only plain rice at camps.

Arrived at Dutch camp at about 1 o'clock and had tea. Made fire and bed but ordered into trucks and moved down to 'regimental camp' where arrived at 4 o'clock. Stayed all day and bought eggs and fish. Fairly good meals.

Buggered about in and out trucks. Left just on dusk and travelled all night.

Train derailed during journey.

22/11/43. Arrived at small station and had breakfast of tinned fish and rice.

14

Return to Singapore

The return journey by train to Singapore which began on 10 December 1943 was much better than the one we had made in April of 1943. For a start, there were only 25 men to each truck, and without exception we all had less than half the amount of gear with which we had left Changi; and the food provided at the various stops was of better quality. Furthermore, the men knew that they were on their way back to a camp in Singapore — where, no matter what the deficiencies might be, the conditions could not possibly be as bad as the camps along the Burma railway. Still, the POW backsides on board that train were as replete with scabies as their packs were devoid of padding, so the trip was not a picnic.

My diary, which I had kept from day to day while we were up on the line, had been sadly neglected since I took sick on December 5, and had to be written up after our arrival back in Singapore. One point noted was the indescribable filth of the men on board our train. As mentioned earlier, the nearest water at Kamburei was over 2 km from our camp, and few had bothered to make the effort of marching all that way for a wash. Our clothes were little more than rags, and few were fortunate enough to have footwear of any description.

The comradeship which had been exhibited on the line was not forgotten on the train, and I thanked God that such a mate as Horrie Ross of our unit was with me in our truck. For the first few days I was still practically helpless, but he saw to my every need and comfort. When we reached one point along the line where latrines had been prepared for the many train-loads of troops returning from Thailand, he helped me out and loaned me his shoulder on which to lean while I made my way to one of the few seats that had been built over the bore-hole.

I began to feel a little better after we had been travelling for two days, and as bananas were available and I still had a few dollars from my working pay, I tried a few of these on my weakened stomach without any dire effects.

We stopped at Kuala Lumpur and Gemas for meals and to stretch our legs. At the Gemas railway station we found the overhead hose that was used to replenish the water supply of the engines. It was probably the first pipe-drawn water that most of us had used to wash ourselves for eight months or so. At least it helped to remove some of the surface dirt and sweat that had accumulated.

We crossed the causeway which joins the mainland to Singapore soon after midnight, and I am sure that every man heaved a sigh of relief to be back on the island, where although they were still to be prisoners of Nippon they would find lots of their mates from whom they had been parted.

We did not learn until we reached Singapore station that we would not be going to Changi but to Sime Road camp, which we had occupied after leaving Adam Park camp in December 1942. We had all hoped that we would be returning to Changi to see our mates once again, but guessed that this pleasure would not be long denied us.

Had there not been transport for all, I was informed by the officer in charge of our truck that I and a few others would be among the few who would be excused the march to the camp. However, approach to the Japanese was unnecessary as trucks were provided for all, and we left the Singapore railway soon after 2 am.

After the inevitable *tenko* on reaching Sime Road camp, we were marched away to our huts. The cooks already in occupation had prepared a meal in readiness for our arrival, and we were soon settled in for the rest of the night. It was a wonderful feeling to be back in a decent camp, where there was electric light, showers, sewerage, concrete paths everywhere, strong huts with either wooden or concrete floors, and a general feeling of cleanliness (apart from our lice-ridden bodies and baggage) about the whole place.

After a few hours sleep, I was up and out to join a few others who had risen early to share the pleasure of washing what few wearable clothes we still had left in our kits. I can still remember how delighted we all were to be able to use the clean running water from the taps at the community wash-stands. It had been my practice up on the railway to wash my shorts in the creek after returning from work each night, and to dry them over the fire in the hut or hang them near my bunk in readiness for work next morning. However, they had not seen water for the past few weeks.

One of the most delightful and satisfying feelings upon entering

Sime Road was to be able to sit peacefully upon a modern and civilised porcelain toilet bowl after squatting down native-style for nine months. The pleasure was all the greater for me in my then state of health.

I went on sick parade that morning, and although I was feeling much improved the medical officer ordered me to remove myself to the camp hospital area to convalesce for a week or two. I was transferred to the malaria ward—exactly the same hut our unit had occupied at the same time the previous year. Before the fortnight was up I felt almost back to normal, though my weight perhaps gainsayed this impression as I must still have been well under 45 kg. However, I was never happy in hospital, so once again I approached the MO to be discharged and was granted permission to return to our unit hut.

By this time it was rapidly approaching Christmas 1943, and although I had covered a few thousand kilometres by train and on foot during the twelve months past, it looked as though my second Christmas as a POW would be spent in the same camp as had my first.

It cannot be difficult for anyone to appreciate how many of our boys treasured the small cards they received through the Red Cross soon after our arrival at Sime Road. These few precious words were, for most of us, the first news we had received from our loved ones since the fall of Singapore in February 1942. For days afterwards men could be seen poring over their small cards from home, the words of which they had long since learned by heart.

Not so fortunate was one chap who learned of the death of his small child. As if this were not enough, the next card he received, a few weeks later, contained the heart-rending news of his wife's passing. Two such blows as these would have been enough to send a man 'off his rocker' under such conditions.

This man had been on the Railway with H Force, and must have endured much to beat 'Dante's Inferno' (now known as Hellfire Pass), the name given to the area on the line where he worked each night. He had not been a very likeable sort of bloke on our first working party at Adam Park in 1942; in fact he was the biggest grumbler I had to contend with. Roll-calls were a bore, work parties were worse, camp duties were to his dislike, and he did not hesitate to say so.

All that was past. He was a new man—not perhaps a happy one, but one we never heard complain—was always on time on parade, among the first to hop in and do a job of work, and showed a spirit which few of us knew he possessed. The change was, to say the least, amazing, and illustrates perfectly that the harsh conditions of the Burma Railway brought out the best in some, and the worst in others.

• • •

Just prior to Christmas, a reorganisation of the whole camp took place. Men had hitherto occupied huts allocated according to the train on which they had arrived from Kamburei. Since the camp now contained Australian, British, American, Dutch and Javanese troops an effort was made to consolidate individual units. The hut to which most of our unit was transferred was situated on a hill overlooking one of the main roads running through the camp and the floor was of wood, and not cement like many of the others. Sime Road camp must at one time have been an excellent peace-time station for members of the RAF, but its appearance and amenities had deteriorated somewhat under the Japanese.

Singapore in peace time was claimed to be a malaria-free island, but this had only been achieved by the constant spraying of streams, canals and drains, and the permanent employment of Tamils to keep down growth of the tall *lalang* grass. However, malaria was now rife on the island and it was necessary to take immediate action to avoid an outbreak on a large scale in our camp.

Parties were sent out each day equipped with native *parangs* and scythes to cut back the long grass and spray the drains in the vicinity of the camp. The Tamils employed by the Singapore Works Department were adept at swinging the scythes in a continual sweeping circle, down to the ground and back up over their heads, but it was not as easy as it looked, as our blokes soon found out. Nevertheless, it was surprising just how much ground could be covered in a day, so that very soon one of the haunts of the troublesome mosquitoes was removed.

Within a few weeks, areas were set aside for the establishment of our own vegetable gardens, and runners of sweet potato, Chinese cabbage, tapioca, paw-paw, etc, were planted out. In the meantime, we had to rely on the ration that Nippon meted out to the camp. The hothouse atmosphere of the island of Singapore made it possible to harvest sweet potatoes and tapioca within a few months of their being planted.

In view of the inadequate supply of vegetables and greens by our hosts, it was always one of the first jobs of men occupying a new camp to seek a suitable spot for a camp garden, and obtain from somewhere the necessary runners, cuttings and seedlings. Quite often the men would start their own gardens close to the huts they occupied, where they could protect their crops from blokes who were low enough to steal them.

It must have been an eye-opener for those civilians who got away from Singapore before the Japanese arrived to find, when they returned after the war, that almost every available plot of land had been put to the cultivation of vegetables. Front gardens, back gardens, land that was actually little more than a swamp, land where once there stood a thriving rubber plantation were cut down now to make a similarly thriving vegetable plantation.

The main Bukit Timah road running from the heart of Singapore city on the south of the island to the causeway joining it to the mainland on the north side has a wide, deep storm channel running along the centre for many kilometres, and this is bordered by a 6 m wide strip of land on either side. The natives living in their hovels used the channel strips along the Bukit Timah road to provide a source of vegetables for their families.

Firewood was in constant demand, and trailer parties were sent out each day to collect and haul back to camp large loads of wood cut down from rubber plantations.

Special gangs were always selected to comprise the forestry unit, as the men had to be capable of cutting and sawing sufficient wood to keep abreast of the continual needs of the camp kitchens. Often the trip would be anything up to 4 km each way over steep and rugged terrain. Fortunately, once the wood had been dragged through the rough wet tracks of the rubber plantations the roads were very good, but the boys were always grateful when they reached the smooth bitumen surfaces where there was no fear of becoming bogged. Quite a distance of the journey back to camp from the rubber plantation was along the road we had helped to build the previous year when we were camped at Adam Park, and all were thankful that it had turned out to be as good as it was.

It was not for several months after our arrival at Sime Road that I was fit enough to qualify for the distinction of belonging to a wood-trailer party. I was by then somewhere in the vicinity of 50 kg. On the return from one of these trips I noticed a Korean guard at the front gate of our camp and recognised the hated Toyama. Presumably he had been demoted since his arrival back on Singapore island, as here he was performing ordinary guard duties. That was the last time I saw him.

In a hut quite close to our own there were a number of Yanks, who had in 1942 come across to Singapore from Java and other parts and had several months later been sent up to Thailand on H Force. Most of them were marines who had been taken prisoner following the sinking of USS *Houston*. The others were lanky members of a Texan Artillery Unit, and a more happy-go-lucky team it would have been hard to find anywhere in our camp. These Americans took their position very philosophically, and when one

entered their hut it was not long before one began to wonder
whether these chaps actually realised that they were prisoners of
war.

I paid frequent visits to their hut, as I had come to know one of
the marines fairly well. He was a short stocky fellow, dark, wore his
Navy cap at a rakish angle and had an air of complete self-assurance.

He was determined to write a book, so I offered to assist by
taking his notes down in shorthand and typing them whenever it was
possible to arrange for the use of a typewriter up at Camp Headquarters during the evening.

Unfortunately our supply of paper gave out long before his story
did, and we had to abandon his impressions of the war, at a stage
where he and his cobbers were trudging along a road in Java after
the sinking of the *Houston* wondering whether the direction they
were taking would land them in territory friendly or otherwise.
Obviously, the result must have been 'otherwise'!

However, I hope that C. P. Fowler of Paducah, Kentucky per-
severed with his writing when he returned to the States, as judging
from his handling of the first few chapters the full story would have
made interesting reading. From what I was told by some of his pals,
he was lucky even to have commenced the writing of a book, as he
had been a very sick man while up on the railway with H Force.

In charge of the Yanks was a bloke named E. A. 'Joe' Bush of
Tulsa, Oklahoma. Joe was a thick-set, rugged type, completely in
command whatever the situation. He was respected and admired by
all his men, and it was easy to see that this esteem was built on his
past record—in the naval actions in which USS *Houston* took part,
and as the men's defender and spokesman in the day-to-day
problems that arose on the line.

The subjects for lectures chosen by men from all walks of life
were many and varied, but attendance following the first night's
delivery depended on its popularity among the listeners. No shadow
of doubt existed about Joe Bush's story of the Sunda Straits action,
as the overflow each night clearly indicated that his audiences would
have sat to listen till all hours had they not been prevented from
doing so by the blowing of 'Lights out', 'All fishing lines in', etc.

Many other speakers gave talks which both entertained and
informed us. There were orations on such varied subjects as 'International Polo', 'Big Game Hunting in India', 'The Australian Test
Tour' (by Ben Barnett), 'Winston Churchill', 'India and Its People',
and 'Cattle Droving in the Northern Territory'.

With us at Sime Road was Bill Williams—a sergeant in the RAF
and a man in a million. He too could keep the interest of his
audience from his first number to the last, and seemed capable of

catering for all tastes. Bill's programs usually consisted of popular songs for which he played his own piano accompaniment, interspersed with a dash of light classical. Bill's skill on the piano, and his lyrical voice, I have described elsewhere in this book. Those who were at Sime Road camp in 1944 will well remember his favourite numbers 'Room 504' and 'If I Only Had Wings'. Later on, the English Concert Party staged an entire program entitled 'Music Through the Ages', with Bill Williams playing and singing tunes made popular over the past 20 to 30 years. It was a great success.

One number the boys were singing at Sime Road was 'I've Got a Lovely Bunch of Coconuts'. Whether the number was written in a POW camp I do not know, but everyone will remember that it was among the hit tunes in the early 1950s — almost six or seven years after we were singing it in Singapore!

In addition to the talented Bill Williams we had with us two brothers who were reputed to have been duo-pianists at the famous Raffles Hotel at Singapore. Their programs usually consisted of classical numbers and considering the type of work they were forced to do with their hands, and the absence of any written music, their performances were really remarkable.

The camp was therefore not short of talent, and it was decided to form a Concert Party to stage nightly entertainment for the troops in a special hut set aside for that purpose. It is no exaggeration to say that some of the plays would have had record runs if the players had had the support of a peace-time population instead of 2000 variety-craving men in a POW camp.

One play I recall very clearly was 'The Rope', which carried an entire cast of English actors. As one can imagine, the acoustics in the hut were not those of a West End theatre, but I doubt anyone at the rear of the hall missed a single word of this gripping drama.

Incredible as it may seem, at times our POW camps contained a 'prison within a prison' — for members of the AIF or British personnel who earned the wrath of the hierarchy for serious or slight misdemeanors. An incident which took place at Sime Road Camp fell into the latter category and involved one Clarrie Tremellan, a member of the 8th Division AASC. He was given five days detention by a court which consisted of Col. Van Den Hoogenbent of the RNEIA, Lieut. Col. Humphries of the Royal Artillery, and Lieut. Col. R. F. Oakes, representing the AIF.

Clarrie was 43 years of age, had suffered cholera and repeated attacks of BT (benign tertain) and MT (malignant tertain) malaria on H Force, and on the day he was arrested was still feeling the effects of a severe bashing received a few days earlier on a wood-trailer party. His explanation for not turning up for a vegetable garden party was not accepted by the tribunal, and he was sentenced to five days in the camp detention barracks. This sentence was ratified by the Japanese Camp Commandant.

The daily ration for barrack prisoners was 310 g of rice, all of those on duty in the barracks were to be addressed as 'staff', and all movements in or around the barracks were to be done at the double! In addition, any breach of barrack orders could be dealt with by the British provost marshal, Lieut. 'Desperate' Dan, who could without further reference to a higher authority increase the term of detention.

It is not surprising that we all wondered how medical officers could make such sacrifices to maintain the health and morale of our men, whilst bastards like 'Desperate' Dan took delight in trying to break them down. It was rumoured later that Lieut. Dan had fallen off a cliff in Southern England!

February 28, 1944 marked the second anniversary of the sinking of HMAS *Perth* and USS *Houston*. It also marked the occasion of our second issue of food through the International Red Cross—the first having been issued in 1942.

The parcels had obviously emanated from the US, as the tinned foodstuffs were all of American manufacture, and the cigarettes 'Camel' and 'Lucky Strike'. In the evening, after the usual *tenko* down on the road fronting our hut, we were issued with one packet of 20 cigarettes per man. Like many others, I had not smoked a cigarette for ages, and felt quite 'heady' after the first few draws on a Camel.

Naturally, our meals took a decided change for the better after the arrival of the Red Cross parcels and the vitamin content in the food meant that many with beri-beri and so on registered immediate signs of improvement. Although much less frequent than deaths on the line we were still continuing to lose a few men each week.

Some of the men who had come down from Thailand in December were still in hospital and their progress, owing to the limited supply of drugs and the absence of good food, was naturally very slow. Many were still suffering from recurring malaria, and others were stricken down with the more serious cerebral malaria. However, the death rate fell as the men in the camp regained some of their strength under the less strained conditions, and those admitted to hospital were assured of excellent attention from the MOs and orderlies who were continuing the job they had started on the railway.

Nevertheless, the cemetery at the front of our camp carried about 50 white crosses before we returned to Changi halfway through 1944.

We had an outbreak of mumps towards the end of April, and I was one of the bunnies to be affected. Mine started with terrific headaches. Although my boots in a haversack were usually soft enough for a pillow, it was now agony to put my head down and I spent the first night walking up and down the concrete path outside our hut. Morning found me on sick parade, and I was admitted to hospital and put in isolation—on a 1.5 m wide verandah, near the door through which most patients walked! At least from my vantage point I could see everything that went on around our hut, which was situated on one of the highest points in the camp. It contained patients mostly suffering from malaria—some serious cases, others in for the umpteenth time with what was now as familiar to them as the common cold.

Although I anticipated that this sojourn in hospital would be brief, it turned out to be the longest that I spent as a POW. I developed an abscess on the backside and it was found necessary to operate, so I was given a 'whiff' and the cause of the trouble removed. The operating theatre was several hundred metres down the hill and I was carried back to my bunk on a stretcher. Major Kevin Fagan performed the operation, which was one way of spending Anzac Day 1944.

I was still in hospital when the whole of our camp was transferred back to Changi in May 1944.

December

30/11/43. Eighteen out of 156 died in train load from No. 3 camp.
    *1/12/43. First party of 500 notified to be prepared to move
tomorrow morning. Sun out today.*
    One man given nine months for stealing blanket.
    *'Paddy' the Irishman suspected smallpox case left at Nicki.
Japanese wanted to either shoot him or bury him alive.*
    Another eleven died on trip down.
    *Eight men at number 3 camp waited for all (patients) to die before
train journey.*
    2/12/43. Party still on parade ground at 12 o'clock.
    Bill Smith arrived from Kamburei Hospital.
    *3/12/43. Went down to river for swim in afternoon and bought
cakes etc. from natives.*
    Used knife and fork for tea (eggs and bread).
    4/12/43. Saturday. Rained all morning. No word of move.
    *5–10/12/43. Very sick. Vomiting and shitting all time and losing
weight very quickly. Hardly able to eat. Had several very nasty turns.
Received very little satisfaction from doctor. Informed by hospital
orderly that had yellow jaundice after about four days treatment at
medical inspection room. Also had malaria at the same time. Lost
almost two stone in about a week.*
    *Party of 600 left Kamburei for Bangkok to be transferred to
Singapore by boat.*
    *10–14/12/43 Feeling very sick on morning of 10th. Taken by
ambulance to station. Only 25 men to truck on this trip. Only 100 F
Force remainder consisting of H Force. Five hundred of F Force
moved to Bangkok a few days previously and reported to be leaving
for Singapore by boat.*
    Had fairly good trip down by train.
    Meals quite good and able to buy bananas etc. — No eggs.
    *Horrie Ross very good to me all way down helped me with
everything.*
    Picked up a little after two days and able to eat.
    Stopped at K.L. and Gemas for meals.
    *Actually a much better trip than up trip in April especially as chaps
only left with small amount of gear.*
    *Men a terrible sight though, with torn clothing and looking filthy
dirty after a few days. Especially after not having washed at
Kamburei. Dirt absolutely engrained into skin.*
    Bathed at Gemas.
    *Arrived at Singapore railway station at about 1.30 a.m. left 2 a.m.
and taken by truck to Sime Road camp.*

15

Return to Changi

T he trip back to Changi was uneventful and quite comfortable, as the Japanese provided us with trucks, which was more than they had done for the 20 km march we had undertaken when Sime Road Camp moved back to Changi in December 1942. However, I was feeling almost as excited as the day we returned to Australia, as it meant that I would be seeing my two pals Jack 'Long Tack' Thompson, and Alf 'Snowy' Macklin. Friendships formed by men in the services can be strong, but none could be stronger than the bond which held the three of us together.

Even though we had been separated for twelve months, my two pals had been in my thoughts each day and in my prayers each night. There were not two finer chaps in the AIF. I had known Snowy since we were at school together; Tack and I formed our friendship from the first days back at Caulfield camp, when he used to fold up my bunk in the morning after finding that it had not been slept in during the night! If ever two POWs were lucky to have a good mate it was Snowy and me, to have Tack. Through four and a half years in Malaya and Singapore, there was not a day went by when Tack was not doing something for either Snowy or myself.

One thing for which I was very grateful was the fact that Jack and Alf had not succeeded in joining F Force when it went to Thailand in April of the previous year. At the time they were both recovering from dysentery and in their weakened condition would have been easily susceptible to further attacks, or even to cholera, had they made the trip.

Fifty-two men comprised our unit quota of F Force, but by the time we returned to Singapore we had lost almost 50 per cent of these. Strangely enough, quite a number of those who died were — like Lex Garner, Norm Lane and Pearce Graham — chaps who were normally over 75 kg and in perfect condition, as well as being younger than many who joined F Force. Death seemed to choose its victims at random, and fate to choose the survivors.

I was turning the thought over in my mind as our truck approached Selarang Square, where I knew Tack would be awaiting our arrival. As we pulled into Selarang Square, I sighted my mate, standing head and shoulders over the other men straining to pick out their unit pals among those standing in the crowded trucks.

Our meeting was as warm as unhappy had been our parting many months before, but we knew in each of our minds that we had not been forgotten.

Snowy could not be there to meet me — I had known that before leaving Sime Road. He had developed an ominous cough several months after F Force left Changi, which turned out to be tuberculosis. He had been in hospital ever since.

Even with the best of treatment, tuberculosis is a grave illness. Imagine the suffering that Snowy went through at Changi camp with its dearth of medication and of plates for the X-ray machines, and food almost devoid of vitamins. Snowy endured these conditions until just three short weeks before we were finally released from prison camp! One is not decorated in the army for attempting to save one's own life, but if they were, Snowy's struggle for survival would place him at the head of the list.

The idea of decorations for POWs has never met with great favour, though all of us recognised that many of our medical officers, and others, had repeatedly forsaken their own safety and health for that of their comrades, and taken all manner of risks comparable to those for which men were often decorated in combatant areas.

What of the medical orderlies who had served among the cholera patients, risking their own lives to save those for whom there was little hope of recovery? What of the medical officers who fought on among the deadly diseases from which their patients were suffering, mindless of the fact that their own strength and health were being jeopardised in the process? Even on the long march in Thailand, what of the mates who risked their own strength by carrying for mile after mile the packs of their pals who were already stricken with disease and debility?

None know better than we, that such men were deserving of the highest recognition, as in the face of very acute danger, they had risked their own safety to save the lives of their pals.

Our stay at Selarang camp was brief, and a week or two after our return we were ordered to shift to Changi gaol a few kilometres down the road.

115 - CHANGI GAOL.

Changi Gaol, 1945. A plan of the gaol is reproduced at page xiii.

The gaol was an imposing building with a high concrete wall surrounding it and a tall tower just inside the entrance. Many of the internal blocks rose to a height of four or five floors, with hundreds of cells in each block. On several occasions the gaol housed 7000 prisoners, and as we were crammed six to a cell intended for one it was no wonder it seemed overcrowded.

Our unit was sent to what we called the 'dungeon'. Our billet was at the rear of one of the main cell blocks, and although the door was of normal size the height of the ceiling from the sloping floor at the rear was no more than 90 cm! In the heat of Singapore the atmosphere was stifling, especially at night when every inch of space was occupied by men trying to sleep. However, we were accustomed to much worse, and only felt pity for the women and children internees who had occupied the same quarters prior to our arrival. Mementos of their presence were inscribed on the white concrete pillars in the 'dungeon': 'Dungeon baby arrived back today', or 'Mary bashed by Japanese guard'.

Rather than sleep in the overcrowded dungeon, many of us sought the fresh air out under the stars, with the cement paths as mattress. Believe me, it was one of the best beds I had as a prisoner especially as any bugs that sucked my already anaemic person were my own, and not those that infested my mates' kits and bedding.

Apart from the 7000 troops who occupied the gaol proper, there were also several thousand men of the infantry battalions billeted outside in the area surrounding it. The main hospital area was also

James Boyle and Jack 'Long Tack' Thompson outside the entrance to Changi Gaol, August 1986.

established outside the gaol in *attap* huts. A few hundred patients were also quartered in what had been the gaolers' living quarters.

Since there were many more of us than there had been civilian internees, working parties were employed all over the camp for many weeks erecting the 70 to 90 m long *attap* huts which we had carted over from Selarang, digging bore-hole latrines, building cookhouses and connecting the electric power.

The gaol cookhouse contained all the modern equipment and facilities necessary to turn out a first-class meal, with dozens of 2 m high ovens, urns that would boil hundreds of gallons of water at a time, and huge rice containers. Unfortunately, such marvels were a little wasted when almost the only ingredient available was rice.

One of the many jobs on which a gang from our unit was employed was the erection of the inevitable barbed wire around the whole area. Under the direction of Capt. Peach of the 2/30th Battalion we were allotted a certain area to be completed by a certain date. Fortunately for us the new fence line passed through a coconut and tapioca plantation, and we were not slow to declare that these would all need to be cleared as we progressed with our barbed-wire entanglement!

The coconuts and the coconut milk, and the 'millionaire's cabbage' inside the trunk of the coconut palm added a much needed appetiser to our meals. The tapioca root was usually shared with mates who had been less fortunate in the job detailed them. Unfortunately the job ran out before our appetites, and we were all transferred to less profitable ventures pulling trailer loads of building materials, digging bore-holes, and assisting with the erection of hospital huts etc.

The gaol had two surrounding walls, approximately 6 m apart; between them ran a cement road. Trucks could thus be driven to the various gaol blocks and could then be admitted through the steel gates placed at intervals around the inside wall. There was only the one main gate at the front of the gaol on the outside wall.

It was whilst pushing a loaded trailer around the gaol road one evening that I foolishly allowed one of the wheels to run over my ankle. It was damned painful, and I was packed off outside to the hospital for examination. About 9 pm I was carried down to the X-ray room, and propped up on a table before the machine. Major Fagan, who had made a preliminary examination earlier, then proceeded to put me through my hoops by twisting and turning the ankle until the sweat was just rolling out of me.

The fact was that there were no X-ray plates to spare for a possible broken ankle-bone when there were many men requiring frequent chest X-rays, so I just sat there whilst my foot was turned in all directions for viewing through the machine.

There were no bones broken, but if there had been the ankle could not have been any more painful, so even with it tied up and propped up in the air in the only real hospital bed I ever occupied in Malaya it was practically impossible to get any sleep. Still, I was not going anywhere in a hurry; in fact, even when I was discharged, I had to hobble around on a stick for several weeks afterwards.

It was during this few weeks' sojourn that I started to transcribe the shorthand notes I had made on F Force. After the working parties had left our lines each morning I would retire to the cool shade of the cement block where I usually slept out at night, and proceed to build on the concise notes I had made from day to day. As was usual, however, the procurement of sufficient note-paper presented its own problems and my meagre supply ran out before very long.

In any case, my ankle healed sufficiently to enable me to report for working parties once again, and within a few days I had joined the 'drome' party—on which most of the Changi POWs were to work from late 1942 until 1945.

The edge of the aerodrome was within a few hundred metres of the Changi beach. A large area of the proposed drome was swamp land, which had to be filled in. The swamp ran parallel to the beach for a kilometre or so, and was bordered on one side by a hill which rose to a height of some 15 m. Out of this hill it was proposed to carve sufficient earth to fill in the swamp, thus creating one straight stretch 2 km or so long, with a similar stretch forming an 'L', at one end of the drome, leading to the headquarters of the Japanese Air Arm.

When I went out to work on the drome for the first time, the job had been under way for over twelve months, and the swamp had been filled in to more than half the level intended. Narrow-gauge railway lines were set down across the drome from the face of the hill, where huge scoops were digging out the earth. This would be loaded into the 'skips' which were then hauled by steam-engine across the drome for us to unload. As soon as the earth had reached a sufficient level in one area the railway lines would be juggled across 6 m or so, and we would start all over again.

More often than not, there was not a breath of breeze and the continual glare from the white surface of the whole area made it very unpleasant. The work was hard, but the hours were shorter than those we had experienced on the railway and there was always the thought that we had a comfortable camp to return to in the evening. There were usually two shifts, one party starting at 6 am and the second completing the day's work at 8 pm.

As hundreds of men were sent from each of the different units in the camp, a team of cooks would accompany each gang and cook their midday meal at the drome. The quality of the meal depended largely on the initiative of members of the cooking teams, as it was their task to gather whatever vegetables or fruit they could en route from the camp to the drome. Quite often, no guard would accompany the cooks along the track, which provided ample opportunity to collect sweet potatoes, tapioca root, etc. from old vegetable gardens.

On one occasion when I was privileged to be a member of the cook's party we gathered quite a few durians from the tall trees in a plantation 2 km or so from the drome. The trees were so big that trying to climb them would have been a very difficult and slow process. However, with stout short sticks thrown with some degree of accuracy we knocked down thirteen in as many minutes.

The fruit, which is the size of a small pineapple, has the toughest skin of any fruit I have seen, with hard sharp points the shape of those of a pineapple. Once the fruit has been cut, its pungent aroma can be detected some distance away.

When we were cutting up our durians for lunch, a Japanese guard decided to come over and examine what was being prepared for lunch. The presence of durians in our vicinity was as plain as the noses on our faces, and trying to keep the aroma from *his* was an impossibility! Fortunately he contented himself with lifting the sack under which they were hidden and taking what he wanted.

The Malays have their own ideas about the merits of the durian. Of this scarce and consequently expensive fruit the saying goes: 'When the durians fall, the sarong rises'. As POWs its efficacy as an aphrodisiac was of small interest to us—what interested us was the bulk it might add to our rations!

16

Orchard Road camp

After a few months working on the aerodrome, I joined another working party which comprised 100 men chosen from four or five AIF units. We finished up at a camp in Orchard Road, in the heart of Singapore city itself.

Whenever working parties were suggested, most of us debated whether it was better to accept 'the devil you knew' than to take the risk of 'copping the crow' as we had all done when we went to Thailand.

The Orchard Road camp was by far the best I was ever in as a prisoner, and I imagine the same was true of the other 99 members. When we reached our new camp, we found three two-storey, newly erected huts, strongly constructed with good timber and three-ply sides. The upstairs section of our hut had solid wooden floors, with raised platforms 3 m wide running down its full length on either side. Our 100 men fitted into one hut quite comfortably—in fact there was room to spare for the first time since we had become prisoners.

The camp also had two large mess-huts, one for us and one for the Japanese. It was surrounded by a high fence, bordered on two sides by large private residences with similarly large grounds; on another, we discovered, by an area of huts filled with Australian three-ply timber, etc. The front of the camp opened onto a back street just off Orchard Road.

There were proper latrines, which were emptied daily by a Chinese contractor. Bugs were the only sign of uncleanliness about the camp, and we could hardly blame anyone else for that, as we had brought them with us! After a few days we were issued with wholestraw pandanus mats on which to sleep, which the Japanese had apparently brought over from Java. In addition to all these good things, the rations were a great improvement on those at Changi and it was not long before we were all beginning to put back some of the weight we had lost.

We were also most fortunate to have with us Terry Wickham, one of the most efficient and popular medical officers in Singapore. Although not a member of the AIF—he was actually in the Indian army—he had cared for our men while he was attached to a camp on H Force on the Burma railway. 'Doc' Terry Wickham was very conscientious, and would go to no end of trouble to help us with the very limited supply of medicines which had been doled out to him before leaving Changi. He was well supported in his work by two medical orderlies, Joe Taylor and Terry Burke.

The officer in charge of our camp was Capt. Hamilton, who had been taken in Timor with Fortress Signals Unit. His 2IC was an Engineer officer, and between them our small contingent of 100 was kept quite happy without the routine and red tape that had punctuated our days back at Changi. Discipline was maintained by W. O. Jim Adams of 8th Division AASC but with his tact and ability to mix with the boys, both as a worker and in their lighter moments, his task was not a very difficult one.

The only other WO in our camp was Charlie Hutchinson, also of the AASC. Charlie was most popular with the boys, a very casual and easy-going sort of bloke and I will warrant he left Singapore without a grey hair in his head! Charlie spent most of his days in camp with sheets of tin, a hammer, and a pair of tin-snips working away to make various containers for the camp and the men. He made me a cylindrical container when the time came to bury my diary and other papers to escape detection in the Japanese kit inspections.

The work we performed during our period at Orchard Road varied from cutting out several acres of a thriving rubber plantation to establish vegetable gardens, to cleaning up the wharves at Keppel Harbour after our bombers had flattened the godowns.

As for the Japanese guards that usually accompanied us on our daily jobs, they were a very meek and mild collection. Most of them appeared to be youngsters recently drafted into the army, and their stay at our camp was short—after which they were probably sent further south to where the fighting still continued.

After passing the Japanese guard at the rear of our camp each morning, they more often than not simply tagged along behind us while we led them to wherever we knew we were going. Apart from the inevitable *tenkos* they hardly ever worried us, which naturally made all of us feel much happier. We more or less worked under our own steam, with one of our own Engineer NCOs supervising.

The most permanent job we had was the establishment of a vegetable garden 24 km or so from our camp, out past Bukit Timah on the Jurong Road. First we had to chop down several hundred rubber trees, grub out the stumps and roots, burn the foliage, then saw the logs and carry them back to the road for transportation back to Singapore. Our bridge-building experiences on the railway had given most of us ample experience of carrying heavy logs, and so long as the balance on the shoulder was right the rest was easy.

We had an old Japanese in charge of our gardens; because of his voice, the boys quickly nicknamed him 'Squeaky'. Old Squeaky showed us how he wanted his garden laid out and within a few short weeks we had thousands of seedlings planted out and thriving in the potash and humus which had been turned into the soil. The heavy rains and hothouse conditions did the rest.

As was to be expected, not all of Squeaky's seedlings went into his gardens. Hundreds of them found their way back to Orchard Road, where Bert Martin and Arthur Penna were forming our own camp garden, in addition to those established by individuals.

My pal Long Tack and I soon established our own little garden plot beside the hut, and some of Squeaky's sweet potato cuttings and seedlings soon enabled us to add a few essential greens to our meals occasionally. The lack of vegetables caused us much concern and sickness at Orchard Road, in spite of the bulk we were receiving in other rations. Our small contingent suffered some of the worst attacks of scrotal dermatitis (Bukit Timahs) and pellagra that I saw among all the men at Singapore.

The dermatitis was of the weeping type, and the affected parts soon became red raw like a piece of meat. It was most painful, and the worst sufferers had to return to Changi for treatment in the skin ward, where they had concocted an effective ointment. What it consisted of apart from the palm oil base I have not the faintest idea, but we knew it as 'alba' and it would cure our complaint within a week or so. Naturally, we never returned to Orchard Road without taking the opportunity to relieve the skin ward of any ointment lying around, so that some at least of our mates were not compelled to return to Changi.

Pellagra was another complaint caused by malnutrition, which affected the tongue and mouth. Those of us suffering this mouth disease were unable to eat food that was in any way solid, or the slightest bit hot. The cooks would dish up 'pap', which was a rice gruel, and after allowing it to become almost cold we would tackle it very daintily to avoid the resultant painful irritation. The only treatment we had at Orchard Road was 'alum' mouth washes.

In order to improve our already comfortable quarters, the Engineer members of our camp began drifting back to camp at night with timber and No. 8 fencing wire which they soon knocked together into wire mattresses hung from the roof. We also felt more entitled to the Australian-branded 3-ply stacked in the godowns, so sheets of this also found their way into camp in the evening or after dark. Cut into suitable sizes, they made excellent draughts and chess-boards, and the latter game would keep the most talkative members silent for hours. Deft fingers and lots of patience carved out some beautiful sets of chess men from the timber we 'discovered' in the godowns.

The 3-ply was ideal for the making of a banjo-mandolin, so having worked out the pattern Long Tack and Max Banks set about producing a source of evening entertainment for me. After the 3-ply, the next problem was to produce suitable strings. The E and A strings were easy, as signal wire served the purpose admirably. However, Ds and Gs were not so simple. We therefore built a machine to produce them. By means of two cotton-reels with bent wire for handles attached to a few pieces of timber, we could complete a full length string in twenty minutes. It was a three-man operation, with two turning the wire handles and the third winding the thin copper coil-wire onto the steel signal wire as it rotated. Quite simple, but most effective, and thanks to Tack and Max I spent many an enjoyable hour lying on my bunk strumming away on my mandolin, playing old favourites.

One tune not recorded in my small notebook of songs (because I did not know its name) was one we used to hear late each night coming to us from private homes just over the high fence surrounding our camp. It was the closing-down tune of the Japanese radio station in Singapore. I did not hear it again for some 30 years after the war, until one evening when my wife and I were dining alone at our home in Rosanna in Melbourne. I put on the turntable a record presented to me on my birthday: 'The James Galway Collection', a selection from Chopin, Schumann, Bach, Rimsky-Korsakoff, and so on. Suddenly, half-way through the record, I heard a haunting melody . . . and rushed to read the wording on the cover. Track No. 4 was 'Song of the Seashore', which meant nothing to me until I read that it was a tune James Galway had picked up on one of his many trips to Japan! Mr Galway must have found the tune as melodious and beautiful as I did, as he later completed a whole album of Japanese tunes which he called 'Song of the Seashore'.

Although our talent was rather limited owing to the small number from which to choose, we attempted to organise several concerts to keep the troops entertained in the evening. With Ken Stocker as compere, Dick Pearce of the Engineers, and a West Australian and myself playing banjo mandolins, 'Shorty' Stidwill and Ken Laity and Doc Davis providing the vocals, and Ken 'Judge' Wild the humorous side of the shows, we gave what was probably a tenth-rate performance, but the boys seemed to enjoy it which was the main thing. We revived the old Adam Park number sung to the tune of 'In eleven more months and ten more days'.

• • •

I doubt that the native population of Singapore ever worried about celebrating Guy Fawkes Day as we usually did in Australia, but on 5 November 1944 they certainly witnessed what was to us POWs a Guy Fawkes Day to remember!

We had, for several weeks previously, been of the opinion that the single plane we could hear but could not see owing to the height at which it was flying was not one of 'ours' (although all planes for the past 3 years had been called 'ours' by the boys).

We were out working in Squeaky's garden when over they started to come in from the west coast, low enough to be visible, B29s flying in beautiful formation: the first Allied planes we had seen since early February 1942, and were we excited to see them again? Wave after wave of them came in, flying in the direction of the oil dumps and naval dockyards, and before long we could hear the 'crump' of their bombs falling.

Naturally, we were too interested in trying to see as much of the show as we could to worry about flying 'shrap' from the ack-ack, and the Japanese and the National Indian gun crews certainly threw plenty of that up to the first invaders of what had been far too long a trouble-free Singapore! At long last, we thought our 'mob' were coming to recover the island and more importantly to get us out of the place. It was almost another twelve months, however, before we could be so lucky—but the bombing raids boosted our morale no end, and rekindled thoughts of home which many of our men had long since abandoned any hope of seeing again.

Several weeks later, we witnessed at first hand the most perfect exhibition of bombing any of us had ever seen. On this occasion, as many men as could be mustered from our little contingent of 100 were detailed to load timber into ships at Keppel Harbour, where all the main wharves and godowns for Singapore island were situated. When we arrived the godowns, which usually extended for 1 km along the wharves, lay flattened or burned down. The godowns had obviously been the target for our boys, and not one bomb had fallen short to land on the wharves themselves.

Many of the godowns had been used to store sheets of rubber baled up and ready for shipment back to Japan, but nothing was left except smouldering heaps. If this raid was a sample of the damage wrought on other targets on the island during the first few weeks of concentrated bombings, Tojo must have been feeling very sorry for himself.

The raids continued at infrequent intervals, and several shelters were dug out of the embankment beside the huts at our camp. One evening when we returned from working in Squeaky's garden we discovered that several men who had remained in camp had been injured during an air raid. They had been taken back immediately to Changi hospital by truck.

One extra commodity issued to us at Orchard Road was a spoonful of sugar with our rice 'pap' at breakfast. As we knew our pal Alf 'Snowy' Macklin to have been transferred to Kranji hospital. Jack Thompson, Alf Ward, Max Banks, Arthur Penna and Berty Martin and myself agreed to forego our sugar ration and send it to Snowy. Charlie Hutchinson would knock up a container with his sheet tin and snips and we knew that Col. Glynn White at Changi would see that the sugar reached Alf safely out at Kranji.

It became increasingly difficult to smuggle letters or notes back to Alf as the kits of any of our sick men returning to Changi from Orchard Road were examined very carefully by the Nip guards. On one occasion, a guard detected some paper used as packing behind a small shaving mirror around which had been sewn some old khaki material to avoid cutting my fingers on the sharp edges of the glass. He ripped it to pieces thinking I had hidden some document or other, but only found an old piece of the Singapore newspaper *Nippon Shimbun!*

All my other valuable papers such as shorthand diary, copies of letters, notes, etc., had been left with one of my pals at Orchard Road prior to my departure for Changi. However, as the pressure was obviously now on in earnest, I decided it would be judicious to dispose of them immediately. 'Hutchy' came to the rescue once again with a cylindrical container, and with old sweated gas cape and rain-cape around the papers on the inside, and then again around the outside, I had what eventually proved to be an air/water tight container. The next job was to find a suitable place to bury it. I selected a spot eleven paces from the doorway of the lower hut, almost against one of the wooden foundation posts. As mentioned earlier, I recovered the papers, intact, eight months later.

None of us was too happy when scrotal dermatitis, pellagra and other diseases caused us to be returned to Changi, but as there were few drugs or ointments at Orchard Road camp there was no alternative. I had to make two trips back to Changi, once to clear up a severe dose of 'Bukit Timahs' and on another occasion to seek an opinion on a peculiar rash which had manifested itself in the vicinity of my buttocks.

It appeared one evening in the form of a long raised weal in the left groin, so I took myself along to Doc Wickham to let him have a peep at it. After instructing the medical orderly to mark it with iodine, he told me to report back in the morning sick parade. However, the 'thing' had disappeared altogether when I rose next morning. Around 10 am I started to scratch at what I thought was a mosquito bite on the right buttock, only to discover this wavy 'worm' about 100 mm long again.

Doc Wickham was very interested and after pumping me with all sorts of questions as to where I had been on the Burma Railway and whether there had been any Burmese in our camp, etc. informed me that he suspected I might have a 'guinea worm' *Dracunculus medinensis*. However, to the best of his knowledge, the complaint had not been detected east of Burma before, so it would be necessary for me to return to Changi with the next party and be examined by the skin specialists there.

The 'worm' would disappear for a week, maybe two then, upon scratching a supposed bite, there it would be again, somewhere else. When the time came to return to Changi the worm was not to be found, and it was not for several weeks after I reached Changi that I was able to present Exhibit A to those that wanted to see it.

After several of the medical officers had seen and discussed it, I gathered from their conversation that they had decided it was not a guinea worm, though I was unable to ascertain at the time, if it wasn't a worm, what in the heck it really was. The rash recurred for many years after the war, but in a much worse form than in Singapore. I suspect that my 'worm rash', in 1944, was the first case of Strongyloides, although it was not for more than 30 years that it was admitted by the Department of Veterans' Affairs in Australia that the rash represented clear evidence of Strongyloides in the system of many ex-POWs.

During the brief visits most of our men from Orchard Road paid to Changi, we took the opportunity whenever we could to obtain tickets to the shows presented by the AIF Concert Party. More often than not demand for tickets exceeded supply, and they had to be rationed out to the various camp areas and units. This was not surprising as these concerts were usually first-class entertainment, and each time a new show was put on, most of the men were not happy until they had seen it.

On one occasion when I was awaiting return to Orchard Road, nobody's baby and naturally not on the list of theatregoers, but nevertheless anxious to see the show, I went to see Syd Piddington, who was in the Concert Party. Some months previously, Syd had been looking for someone to type out copies of the script of 'Autumn Crocus', which they intended to produce. I had finished up doing the job for him on the back of old criminal records that had been found at the gaol.

Syd could not promise any front-row stalls, but two of us managed to see the whole show from the catwalk above the stage. The stage incidentally was a tremendous affair, elaborately decorated, and with an assortment of backdrops appropriate to anything from the ballroom scene of 'Cinderella' to the wood in 'A Midsummer Night's Dream'.

When one considers that the Changi Concert Party launched the careers of men such as Syd Piddington, now known worldwide for his mental telepathy acts; John Woods, who appeared in several Australian stage performances; and Frank Rich, the radio comedian and singer, it is not difficult to appreciate the high standard of the many concerts presented for the benefit of the troops in Changi.

This standard was only maintained by the constant practices and rehearsals upon which their producer insisted. All members of the Concert Party were more or less free of ordinary camp duties, and would have found themselves very quickly among the workers if their popularity waned.

Gambling was a diversion that was frowned upon by Japanese and our officers alike. 'Swi' (two-up) was banned in every area of the camp, but naturally one could find at least two games somewhere in the Changi area if one was sufficiently interested. One of our blokes was always particularly interested in a game of 'swi', had been ever since we knew him first at Kubu Park, Malacca in 1941, and probably still is. A game of two-up was like a magnet to 'Pop' Minnis from Southern Cross in Western Australia and as soon as the evening *tenko* was over, he would set out to locate it. As was to be expected, Pop often returned at 'lights out' with a huge pile of notes — and on other occasions, stone-motherless-broke. However, Pop was always equipped to make a 'comeback' as invariably when he was over-capitalised he would stock his larder with readily saleable tinned or fresh foodstuffs and when the necessity arose he would sell sufficient to enable him to raise a bank with which to 'back the tail' again.

Pop was aptly called 'Minnis the Menace', as he ruined more 'swi' games in Changi than any other man would have been game to. It was said that if Pop could not get 'set' — place a bet — to his satisfaction, he would even go so far as to 'lay the odds'. This means that he would offer 'two to one' to induce others to bet. It is a most unorthodox way of playing two-up and frowned upon in most games. He was known to all the camp provosts and eventually certain areas of the camp were placed 'out of bounds' to him, but Pop was such a cagey little coot I doubt that this had any effect upon his activities.

The camp provosts were a constant source of worry to lots of us, as it was bad enough being prisoners of the Japanese without having these bludgers patrolling the camp. The provosts were always on the alert to catch the 'ring-keeper' of any game, and they would have to toe the carpet and perhaps do seven days in the jug if caught.

The efforts of one provost at least were frustrated at a time when he was probably all set to 'make a kill' on a game in progress in the hospital area. A Japanese guard happened to be standing near the *attap* hut behind which this particular provost was creeping up on the big game. The guard apparently realised what the provost was intent on doing. With a grunt and a *kurrah* the Japanese guard brought him to a speedy halt, and stood him to attention in his tracks. At the same time, the guard ordered a passer-by to go on up to the game and warn them to break it up. This Japanese probably felt the same contempt for the Japanese *Kempei-Tei* as we did for the provosts. Anyhow, it was as good a turn as I ever heard any Japanese doing for our blokes.

There were also many at Changi who became deranged under the strain of captivity. One bloke I knew quite well, and who had been one of the stretcher-carrying party with me between Shimo Sonkurei and Kami Sonkurei back in 1943 on the Burma railway became completely insane. At times he would grab all his cobbers' mess dixies, set them out on the floor of their quarters, and then stand back and give them drill instruction. On other occasions he would stand on the road watching the Japanese guards marching by, then run after them and hop into the blank file and march off down the road, completely happy.

One poor bloke who was completely nuts attempted to commit suicide by jumping down a 6 m bore-hole latrine. If there was any humour in this incident it was expressed by one of his fellow inmates in that section of the camp hospital, who remarked: 'He ain't mad. If he'd been mad, he would have gone in head first'!

I eventually returned to Orchard Road camp when there was sufficient of our boys to warrant a special trip back from Changi. Soon after my return, my pal Tack (Jack Thompson) became dangerously ill and had to be sent back to Changi immediately. He finally contracted a sort of paralysis of the legs and was for months afterwards walking around on sticks.

His illness began one morning when we were on the small parade-ground outside our hut, awaiting the Japanese guards to

Alf 'Snowy' Macklin's grave at Kranji Cemetery, Singapore island.
Photographed August 1986.

take us to work. Tack complained of feeling off-colour, and I
insisted that he report back to 'Doc' Terry Wickham, who promptly
ordered him into bed.

That night Tack was really bad, delirious and in a high state of
fever. Naturally, I was very worried about him, but there was little I
could do apart from trying to make him as comfortable as possible,
and trying to ease his mind during his frequent spells of delirium.

I had already had sufficient experience of blokes on the railway suffering from similar types of fever, and the fact that most of them had soon died did not make me feel any happier. Fortunately, Doc Wickham and Capt. Hamilton were able to arrange a special trip to take Tack back to Changi. It was a great blow having to farewell Tack after our twelve months at Orchard Road together. It was not until October 1945, when Tack arrived at Spencer Street railway station, Melbourne that we met again.

After a few months recuperating at Changi, Tack had gone out to Kranji to be with our other pal Alf 'Snowy' Macklin, who was still suffering from tuberculosis.

Tack could easily have come back to Orchard Road where he knew conditions to be far better than either Changi or Kranji hospital camps. No other man in Changi would have sacrificed this opportunity to return, but Tack knew that Alf needed him and asked to be sent out to Kranji.

Alf died three weeks before we got out of Singapore, but had he lived, one man would have been responsible. Tack would sacrifice his pay, scrounge any article of clothing that might make pyjamas, keep any sugar or other scarce commodity, repair his bed-sheets, make him pillowcases, and read to him when he was too weak to hold a book himself; Alf had but to make the slightest request, and were it humanly possible to obtain it in Singapore, Tack would turn heaven and earth to get it.

When things were tough up in Thailand and Burma, comradeship among our men became very strong, but no mate's individual effort ever surpassed that of Tack's, whose friendship and thought for Alf persisted until the bitter end. Cols. Charles Osborne and Cotter-Harvey were two of the medical officers attending Alf, and I feel sure they did not underestimate the value of Tack's efforts to obtain his recovery.

One of the last jobs we had to perform for the Japanese before leaving Orchard Road camp was to dig drains for sewer pipes at a new camp they were building quite close to the Alexandra Hospital. It was here that the Japanese massacred nearly all the patients during their occupation of Singapore in February 1942.

Our job was rendered all the more difficult because the Japanese had already built their latrines — instead of first choosing an elevated spot and taking advantage of the natural fall of the land, they had chosen one of the lowest spots. The result was we had to dig our drains about 3 m deep before we started and considering the sum of 10 cents a day we were being paid, Cpl. Laurie Coxall's wry remark that we were just 'digging for . . .' could not have been any closer to the truth.

We were on this job for many weeks before it was finally completed, but considering we were not a large party, and the drains were altogether about 120 m in length, the progress was quite good. It was blazing hot and, digging at that depth, it was no wonder the sweat flowed by the cup-full. Trying to toss out the earth in such a confined space presented its own problems when we approached the final depth — if you did not throw high enough you were invariably showered with dirt as it fell back.

I copped a dose of lumbago, probably due to the sweat and the cold draught which often blew down the length of the deep drain. After a couple of days off, I reported back to Doc Wickham that I was quite okay and went back to work. However, after a few hours the pain returned with much more severity, so Doc Wickham confined me to bed again, and told me to stay there until he ruled me fit and not before. As I could hardly move without extreme pain, I was quite happy to leave the decision to him!

The Japanese apparently had their own hospital at Alexandra, as we saw some of the Japanese nurses there. By comparison to the trim neat uniforms of the Australian nurses, they looked like little plump balls of white with a sash tied around the middle!

We were quite resigned to spending the remainder of our POW days at Orchard Road, but we learned with regret that we were to move back to Changi. At Orchard Road we must have been under the control of a Japanese HQ that was efficient in most respects, as the camp was much better administered than any other we occupied, and the Japanese always tried to satisfy the demands of our own camp commanders.

On the day of our departure they provided sufficient trucks for all men and their equipment, and for a while at any rate we said goodbye to Singapore city and returned to the depressing shadows of the Changi gaol.

* * *

Changi in 1945 had long since established a monotonous daily routine. Reveille, breakfast of rice-pap, parade for working party in the camp gardens, 'drome' details, trailer parties, sick-parades, hospital trailers, bore-hole digging, lunch, more working parties in the afternoon, evening meal, *tenko*, and visiting mates in the hospital area or attending one of the camp concerts. Apart from the news bulletins that were still being received on the camp wireless there was little of interest.

Most of the men who returned with our party from Orchard Road were in fairly good condition, and we were quickly roped in to make up the numbers for the toughest of the Changi assignments. Among these were the trailer parties to collect wood for the various cookhouses, which were catering for 7000 inside the gaol alone. Outside the gaol were billeted some of the infantry battalions, plus the whole of the camp hospital, and they burned quite a few tonnes of wood each day. The trailers were actually not so very old trucks, from which the engines and all else had been removed leaving the tray bodies only. The steering-wheels of course and sometimes the brakes remained, but the latter were not always in A1 condition and it was usually advisable to heed the cry of 'mad driver—no brakes'.

The area around Changi was not exactly flat but the main bitumen roads were still in good condition allowing our trailers to gather fairly reasonable speeds when we were rolling down the long hills with a heavy load. The hills of course also had their drawbacks as it was pretty tough going pulling a heavy trailer up the long steep slopes.

We usually left Changi gaol about 8.15 am with 20 men in the tracers of three or four trailers. The majority, but not all of us, had boots, but anyhow you could always get a better footing on the road in bare feet, and as none of us was exactly tender-footed it made little difference.

The first half kilometre or so was comparatively flat going, and we had to pull the trailers until we reached the start of a down-gradient, when the trailers would stop, the traces be dragged back on to the truck, and everyone would scramble aboard. Then would commence the free-wheel ride, rolling down the hill as fast as she would go, finally levelling out on a flat stretch, but so long as there remained an ounce of momentum no-one would attempt to climb down.

As soon as each trailer party had a full load they would make their way out over the boggy plantation to the bitumen road and wait for the other trailers to complete their loads. Usually we had time for a smoke before commencing the long drag back.

Certainly we had bitumen roads and rubber-tyred trailers, but we also had the dead weight of three or four tonnes to pull the full distance back to camp, and if you had not been on a trailer party for a while your blistered hands would testify to the fact.

Anyone could lean on a shovel or a 'chunkle' with the best of the bludgers and get away with it, but there was no room for shirkers in the traces. There were four men on each cross-bar of the trace, one pair pulling against the other pair and their combined effort pulling the trailer. If one of the four slackened off, it upset the even pull and was fairly obvious to the others in the team. In such case, the would-be 'lead-swinger' became the subject of a volley of well-directed oaths like 'bend your back you bastard' which soon brought him back into line.

Naturally, some teams and some trailers were better than others and could make quicker times on the long pulls up some of the steep hills, so that there was a wait for the others to catch up. In order to make the most of this advantage, leads were usually planned for places where it was possible to scrounge some tapioca roots or sweet bucks (potatoes) from the gardens adjoining the road.

We soon learned the best spots for our scrounging, and endeavoured to arrange that the Japanese guard would be accompanying one of the trailers at the rear. By adoption a 'go-slow' policy, the men on the first trailer would have sufficient time to collect a good bag from the nearest garden. Strange as it may seem, private cooking in camp was an offence, so in addition to getting our extra rations past the Japanese guards it was necessary to escape the snooping of our own camp provosts.

Among the British troops at Changi was a padre named Duckworth, a stumpy, fair complexioned, and happy-go-lucky chap who endeared himself to the men of all nationalities. He was in fact so different from all the other padres that the boys often wondered how on earth he ever came to attach himself to the ministry. Nevertheless, he did a grand job as a morale-builder. When the horrors of Singapore have been forgotten, the humour will still be remembered by those men who shared in it, and Duckworth's name will certainly be associated with those memories.

For some reason best known to himself, Duckworth displayed a distinct dislike for anyone who wore 'pips' on his shoulders. It was his habit to open his lecture on 'Boat Racing with Cambridge' by saying to his usually large audience: 'Gentlemen—I presume there are no officers present'! Perhaps it was because the ORs shared his sentiments, that they accepted him as 'one of the boys'.

One of my most vivid memories of the Changi gaol is of one very bright moonlight night when I was returning to the gaol just before 'lights out'. The night air was still, and as I strolled down the cement road between the two high walls I could not help but feel how peaceful it was. Faintly, there drifted to me the strains of Beethoven's 'Moonlight Sonata' and as I walked on I could see at the bottom of the road a Javanese, sitting at a piano in the bright moonlight playing in what must surely have been the most serene setting ever dreamed of since Beethoven first composed his masterpiece. The atmosphere was perfect, and no doubt it was because of this, that our Javanese friend felt the desire to sit and play.

Although I have heard the 'Moonlight Sonata' many times before and since, never has it sounded as beautiful as that night at Changi gaol in 1945.

We were kept well-acquainted with activities in other theatres of war, and in the early stages of the year our interests were naturally centred around the movements in Europe, where it appeared the Germans were now being pushed back. The news of course meant to us the first real turn of the tide, as few of us expected that Nippon would be able to hang on for long once the Germans were defeated. But we still had several months to cool our heels on Singapore island. Fortunately, by that stage we were almost immune to disappointments. We had become so sceptical of all reports that when we were finally awakened one night with the news that victory was ours, many men in Changi simply passed a few rude remarks about being just another so and so furphy and rolled over and attempted to go back to sleep.

In the meantime, however, the Japanese continued to call men for various working parties, and of course there was always plenty of work to be done around Changi. Several men were more or less permanently employed at the Changi cemetery, keeping the gardens and the graves tidy. The cemetery lay right at the end of the main road from Singapore, within a stone's throw of the huge airfield we had been building for several years. The men employed at the cemetery were both of our own unit, and had served in World War I. Frangipani trees fringed the road and entrance, and inside the gates the atmosphere was one of greenness and serenity, with graves and crosses immaculate and perfectly aligned.

It was a long march down to the cemetery, and a hot one for those attending a burial service, as these were the only occasions apart from church parades when anyone in Changi ever dreamed of wearing more rather than less.

Toward the end of our captivity we were forced to find another site for a cemetery, possibly because the original one was too close to the airfield. The only burial service I attended in Changi was just after we were liberated. It was one of the most tragic deaths in Changi's infamous history, caused by the victim's own hand in his insatiable craving for food.

Even in our early days at Adam Park in 1942, this chap would eat banana skins and so on, but the diet he forced upon himself just prior to his death consisted of raw coffee beans, about 3 kg of tapioca root, and sugar. Tapioca root was one of the few foods readily available and he could not resist the temptation to satisfy his craving for bulk. So far as I can remember he was the last man in our unit to die before we left Changi a few weeks later.

Memories of Singapore are studded with either the most tragic or humorous moments. We can still laugh when we remember the little Japanese down on the drome who told the boys that instead of him knowing 'bugger nothing' as they thought, he knew 'bugger all'! The

Japanese at Adam Park who answered 'boom-boom' to almost every city in Australia the boys named—including Luna Park! The petrol old Bill Cummins drew from the Japanese engineers to start the steam-rollers!

Many will remember the 'Yank' at Bukit Timah camp (an American–Japanese forced into the army as an interpreter when on a short visit to Japan), who told our boys on parade that if they wished to return to Australia they should cease stealing Japanese petrol and selling it to the Chinese. The 'Yank' discovered upon return to his own little sports car that the boys had 'milked' his tank!

On one occasion the 'Yank' was driving a utility truck back to Singapore from a work camp at Bukit Timah with a couple of our blokes standing in the back. One of them remarked to the others: 'I wonder if this little Japanese bastard will stop at the coffee-shop and let us have a drink'. The 'Yank', who was then unknown to them apparently, popped his head through the little window and said in his Yankee drawl: 'I'm no Japanese bastard and we are not stopping at any coffee-shop'!

17

He ain't heavy, he's my mate!

After a few months at Changi, the Japanese called for men for a further working party. Our area of the camp was selected to make up the required number, and I was among those chosen from our unit. We did not know where we were being sent, but it was good to get away from Changi once again, as I for one thought there were too many bludgers and no-hopers there. As was to be expected, the usual ones had all sorts of excuses to keep them off the draft.

We left Changi by truck and soon gathered that we were making for the west coast. After turning off one of the main roads we made our way through some heavily timbered rubber plantations to a well-guarded camp, completely encircled by high barbed wire entanglements. The Japanese were taking no chances of any of us escaping at this stage.

The camp area was poor, and unlike Orchard Road no preparations appeared to have been made for our arrival. Cookhouses had to be erected, water-pipes obtained, and the nearby creek dammed to give sufficient pressure to get water to our cookhouses, etc. Latrines had to be dug, and a hut erected for the RAP and 'Doc' Terry Wickham, who we were once again fortunate enough to have with us.

The Japanese engineers and guards were a nasty crew, but we soon learned that several groups of Koreans were also attached to this camp. They were stationed at several spots a few kilometres from the main camp. The attitude of these Koreans towards us, and towards the Japanese was a complete reversal of their attitude on the Burma railway. We were unaware of the motives for the Koreans' looking on us with favour, but were quick to take advantage

174

of the situation and frequently took liberties we would not previously have thought possible.

Of course, we still had to work, and hard work it was. The Japanese were preparing for an invasion from the west coast, and it was our job to build anti-aircraft and gun emplacements, and dig tunnels into the east side of all the hills in the surrounding area. All day long we would toil, carting heavy timber for the reinforcing of the maze of gun emplacements we were building on the tops of the steep hills. The Japanese appeared to think that the work was a matter of some urgency, and constantly urged our blokes to greater efforts. Quite often we would return to camp in darkness, and Reveille was always before dawn.

Apart from the gun emplacements, which were quite close to the camp area, most of our jobs first entailed a march of anything up to 4 km. A large section of the march required our party to move in single file along a narrow path through scrub and numerous vegetable gardens. Parties sent out for each job usually numbered about nine men, as in the confined space of the tunnels we had to excavate it was impossible to accommodate more than a few at a time.

We soon learned the spots along the track where we might scrounge some sweet potatoes, tapioca root, or pineapples. According to a pre-arranged plan, the men at the rear of the file would lag behind while those at the head would walk faster—giving them time to rush into the vegetable gardens, stuff their haversacks with whatever they could and be back on the track before the Japanese guard caught up.

One of our favourite spots was just past a wire fence we had to crawl through. The first few men through were always quickest, rounding a bend a few metres further on and shooting off into the gardens. Of course the remainder got themselves thoroughly tangled up in the barbed-wire in an effort to delay the Japanese guard who was given the privilege of crawling through last.

If Nippon was not going to feed us properly we had to find ways of doing so ourselves. We felt that the Chinese to whom the gardens belonged would willingly have given us some of their vegetables— had the Japanese not made it clear for many years that they were not to help POWs.

On some days our efforts were frustrated by the inclusion of a second guard who would march at the head of the column. However, by trailing the rear of the party and speeding up the head, the men in the middle would grasp any opportunity that presented itself. Knowing the ration usually doled out to us for our midday meal, the risk was always worth it.

Upon arrival, the guard would report to the Japanese NCO in

charge of the area, our men would line up and number off from the right in Japanese *ichi, nee, san* — and within a few minutes we were back at work. Our little gang consisted of Max Banks, Dave Cupples, Ernie Fixter, Olly Frost, 'Scotty' Allen, and a few others from another unit.

The Japanese had decided to build 'rat holes' into the east side of the hills, and these consisted of two parallel tunnels about 6 m apart, and linked at right angles after they had been driven about 10 m into the side of the hill. The entrances were about 1.5 m high, and this necessitated digging an approach before commencing the actual tunnelling.

It was apparently the intention of the Japanese to store ammunition in the tunnels we were digging, and in the event of an invasion to fall back on the dumps. Our efforts proved futile, however, as Nippon capitulated before we had completed many of the tunnels.

The last day we spent on the job was one that all of us will remember. More often than not, our little party was given either rations or gear to take out to the Japanese quartered near our job, which was about 4 km from camp. On this particular morning, we had about 90 kg of rice to lump, and as it was raining in typical Malayan fashion, our trip was not as fruitful as usual!

When we arrived we found the Japanese sergeant in charge of the area had taken up quarters on our job, and he was not in a happy frame of mind. The sergeant informed us that Chinese would, from that morning, be carrying on with the tunnels and that our party would be carting timber and old railway lines from the main road, a distance of several kilometres along a bush track.

In spite of the pouring rain, which lasted for about four or five hours, we were ordered to take two small two-wheeled mountain carts, and start off for our first load — four men to each cart. Of the whole party I think I was about the most fashionably attired, in a pair of badly worn and leaky boots, an old Pommie battle-dress jacket and a 'giggle' hat. Of the remainder, one had a decent pair of boots, most of the others none at all, two had old rice bags around their shoulders, and all of us had shorts that were tattered and worn — we were as cold as frogs, and just as miserable.

We successfully accomplished the first trip before lunch, having hauled fifteen iron rails, each weighing well over 50 kgs on each of the two carts. Several times, one of the carts became bogged in the mud and we had to call on the full strength of our eight men to drag it out. The carts kept swinging from side to side on the rough track, jarring our hips as the bars crashed against them.

After a lunch of plain rice and tapioca/blachan stew we departed for another load, the rain still pelting down. On the return journey, however, we met with disaster. Pulling up a slight slope, through thick heavy mud, one of the men in the leading cart who was already in a weak condition had a complete black-out, slipped, and struck his head heavily on the ground.

I told the guard we would have to get him back to camp immediately, and fortunately struck a native driving his yak cart along the track. I detailed off L.Cpl. Olly Frost to accompany him back to camp and after lifting him on to the yak cart, we set off to complete the journey with three men to a cart.

Our job was difficult enough with four men, but the task was well-nigh impossible with three. We expected that when we returned from the second trip the Japanese would call it a day, or at least put the six men on the one cart—but we were to be disappointed. After a smoko we were ordered to return for another load—with three very weary men to each cart. Our shoulders were aching, our arms had been nearly pulled out of their sockets with the twisting and turning of the bars on the front of the cart, and we were covered in mud from head to foot.

We were exhausted when we finished our last load just on dusk, and to make matters worse another of our small party collapsed before we could start our march back to camp. Most of us in that small party had worked on the Burma railway, and 'Scotty' Allen had been among the sickest who had been transferred to Tambaya hospital to recover. Scotty was a good mate and a good worker who was a welcome member of our small daily party of mostly 4th MT. He had collapsed from sheer exhaustion after a gruelling day in the pouring rain. After a short rest and a 'cuppa', and because there was no other means of transport, I piggybacked him the 4 km or so back to camp.

Before we left however, and without seeking a reason, we were more than pleased to learn that the next day was to be a *yesame* (holiday). The atmosphere in the camp when we returned seemed strangely portentous; the Japanese guards had been doubled and there were hints that all the men would be returning to Changi. Next morning, soon after breakfast, the rumour became fact, and we were packed up and ready to move out before 10 am while the Japanese immediately began stacking bags of rice in the huts we had just vacated.

The atmosphere was electric, and we all realised that some very important developments must have taken place during the past twelve hours. Then a Chinese worker whispered the news through our bamboo fence that Japan had surrendered. We were all reluctant to accept the news for which we had waited for three and a half years, but this time the moves afoot in the camp certainly seemed to offer a dangerous hope that it might, at last, be true.

Some of our men, however, later said that they had the impression we were being lined up on the road to be shot, and this could well have proved to be the case, as it was revealed later that orders had in fact been issued in other areas for such action to be taken in the event of an Allied invasion!

Although the world was not yet aware of the announcement, 11 August 1945 was when we heard the stupendous news! What is more, it was Tack's 25th birthday! It is not likely that he has received a more welcome birthday present either before or since.

18

Liberation

Changi, the POW nerve centre and human 'stock exchange' from which all news and furphies emanated, was transformed over-night. Chaps who had previously been moping about with a hang-dog look and a no-hoper attitude, were now convinced that their days as POWs were numbered.

In spite of searches by Japanese guards at unexpected hours of the day and night and threats of reprisals in the cutting off of heads and the cutting down of rations, our 'canaries' which were expertly hidden in walls, cookhouses, brooms, operating theatres and so on continued to operate.

When in the early hours of the morning of Sunday—August 12—the news was received, the report soon spread around the camp, and mess orderlies were instructed to report to the gaol kitchen, complete with tea-buckets, to collect the good news.

The lights were turned on throughout the camp and for those who still doubted the report, a quick trip to the cookhouse could confirm that a responsible officer was handing out the news that the war was over, Nippon had capitulated, and we as POWs were now free men.

To hundreds of our sick cobbers in hospital the news gave a new lease of life, especially to those who had been nearing the end. Of course, there were many who were beyond hope of recovery and who, in spite of all efforts, passed on during the few weeks before our eventual release.

Because the news had only reached us by way of our illicit radios, we continued in the normal way, digging new vegetable plots and doing maintenance work around the camp. The Japanese HQ kept us in ignorance, but the Japanese and Korean guards gradually began to impart the startling news of the surrender of Nippon.

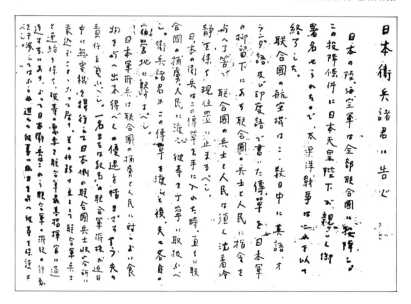

Instructions to Japanese guards.

The land, sea and air forces of Japan have completely surrendered. Tenno Heiko has personally ordered capitulation, and the Pacific war is over. In a few days United Nations planes will be dropping orders written in English, Dutch, Malay, to United Nations soldiers, and civilians, in the hands of Japanese Forces.

The United Nations civilians, soldiers, etc. should remain calm, and remain in their present positions.

When these pamphlets come into the hands of Japanese guards, they must hand them over to United Nations prisoners and civilians, and treat them with care.

After handing over pamphlets, guards must return to their barracks.

Japanese officers and guards are to treat prisoners with care, and give them as much good food as they may require.

This is their responsibility. Within a few days, United Nations officers will come to internment camps with transmitting sets of transmit the needs of prisoners and civilians to the Supreme Commander of the United Nations.

The Japanese guards must not interfere with these officers, but should help and protect them.

Pamphlet dropped by Allied planes over Changi Camp at 3 pm on 28 August 1945.

Records Office,
Victoria L. of C. Area,
281 Lonsdale St.,
MELBOURNE, C.1.

78/19/283   25th June, 1945.

Mrs. **Edith** Pascoe,
5, Love Street,
HARTWELL.

Ref:-   VX 45598 - CPL. BOYLE, J.

It is advised that in a message broadcast by Japanese
radio from S'PORE   on 11/5/45 a member of the Australian
Imperial Forces is alleged to have stated that

"JIM, JACK, SELF WELL"

The name mentioned in the message would appear to
refer to the above named soldier, and the information is
conveyed to you with the warning, that in view of the nature
of its receipt and that it emanates from an enemy source it
should be accepted with reserve.

Yours faithfully,

[signature]

Lieut.Col.,
Officer in Charge, Records.

URGENT

COMMONWEALTH OF AUSTRALIA.
POSTMASTER-GENERAL'S DEPARTMENT.
TELEGRAM

The date stamp indicates the date of reception and lodgment also, unless an earlier date is shown after the time of lodgment.

Office Date Stamp.

3 SEP 1945

URGT 131 MELBOURNE 36/1 11A

MRS E PASCOE   *131*

5 LOVE ST HARTWELL

IT IS ADVISED THAT VX45598 BOYLE J DEPARTED SINGAPORE FOR SYDNEY
ON TWELFTH SEPTEMBER 1945 BY AIR FURTHER ADVICE AS AVAILABLE
...VICTORIA ECHELON AND RECORDS 281 LONSDALE ST MELBOURNE

(5 1945 281)

Two of the messages sent to James Boyle's sister, Edith, during 1942 to 1945.

Ours was the first working party to return to Changi, but the following few days saw parties returning from all parts of Singapore island, Johore Bahru, and outlying islands off Singapore. All told of the difficult work they had been forced to perform during the latter few months, and the extremely long hours (at least twelve hours a day), which had resulted in many being admitted to hospital.

A few days after our return to Changi, a civilian car was seen to pull up at the main entrance and out stepped two chaps dressed in civilian clothing. They reported to our own picket at the main gate and related the almost unbelievable story that they were actually marines from HMS *Repulse*.

Since the fall of Singapore in February 1942, they had been posing as civilians and had been employed as mechanics at a garage in Singapore. They had claimed to be Eurasians, but as soon as they heard the good news they admitted to the Japanese that they were English and disclosed their real identities.

'It was amazing to see the startled look on the faces of the Japanese when they finally realised what we were trying to tell them', said one of the marines. The Nip in charge grew quite excited, and as the light of understanding began to dawn upon his face, he screamed out 'You Englishmen—all Englishmen Changi'. He immediately proceeded to hustle the two marines into a car, and they saw the inside of a POW camp for the first time in three and a half years—after the war was over.

Toward the end of August, the Japanese began to pour supplies of Red Cross food into our camp. These were brought from godowns in Singapore, where the Japanese had stored them in packing cases since 1942. Naturally, it was foolish to start devouring food in large quantities, in spite of our hunger, as the affect would undoubtedly have been disastrous.

On August 28, pamphlets were dropped by Allied planes which flew very low over Changi, and they informed our hosts that the war was over and instructed them to give us food, care, etc. and to await the arrival of United Nations officers, who were due to arrive at Singapore within a few days. Pamphlets printed in English were also dropped the same day to our own troops and these warned us of the dangers of over-eating!

These pamphlets represented the first tangible contact with the outside world in nearly eighteen months since the last batch of Red Cross mail, although in actual fact it would be safe to say that we had been cut off for almost three and a half years.

The dark days of misery were, I thought, now gone, but fate was still to play its trump card so far as Jack and I were concerned. A party returned from Kranji hospital camp toward the end of August,

These photographs cover some of the ceremony which took place prior to the signing of the surrender document in Singapore on 12 September 1945. Lord Louis Mountbatten, as Supreme Commander of Allied Forces in the Far East, insisted that this surrender be quite separate to the American-arranged ceremony. Top: *Lord Louis and party.* Bottom: *Japanese General goes to sign.*

and brought the news that our pal Alf 'Snowy' Macklin had died. Billy Cook of our unit tried to break the news to me as easily as he could, but it was impossible to realise that now we were free men, Alf would not be returning home with us, and I just sat in a half-stupor wondering why it should be. For the first time in many years I could not control the tears that came to my eyes, as Alf meant as much to Jack and me as our own brothers.

Jack was, of course, still out at Kranji, and the following morning I received the note which he had written to tell me of Alf. Jack had not left his side during the last week, and the severe blow must have been doubly hard to bear when just three short weeks later he learned that we would now be returning to Australia.

Both Jack and I had known that there was little hope of Alf being cured while we were still POWs on Singapore island, but we had always hoped when the day did come to return home, we would be able to take Alf with us. Alf was one of the bravest men any POW doctor attended, and the suffering he endured for so long without complaint made those who attended him give of their utmost in an effort to equal the fighting spirit they saw in him.

Doctors and men alike were amazed that with little or no treatment available, food of the lowest vitamin content, and the poorest of hospital conditions, Alf hung grimly for so long to the little life that was left in his body.

• • •

I had hoped that before leaving Singapore it would be possible to make a trip out to Kranji to see Alf's grave, but as no official party went there from Changi, I had to see what I could do on my own. It was a 50 km return trip to Kranji, and as transport was nonexistent, the task did not look very hopeful.

Fortunately, few restrictions were now placed on our daily movements, so one morning I set forth in the direction of Singapore to see if I could get out from the city itself. As the city was a 30 km walk from Changi, it was almost lunch time before I arrived, and here again no transport was available.

Without money to offer, no one would listen to my request to be taken to Kranji, so I set off for the dock area where some of our ships were reported to be berthed. By this time quite a number of our boys had found their way into the city and among them were a couple I knew, including Horrie Ross of our unit. We boarded the warships and were given some food, and told of the place along the wharves where some of their tinned foods, partly damaged, had been dumped.

We soon found the dump, and our eyes lit up when we saw tins of fruit, milk, butter and so on which were ours for the taking. With a 30 km march back to Changi ahead of us we could not take very much, however we half-filled a rice sack and, as Horrie was in no fit state, I heaved it on to my back.

It was heavier than I expected, and after a short while I realised that I could not possibly cart our welcome prizes all the way back to Changi. However, we had ample ammunition in the rice sack to barter with any taxi driver for a lift back to camp. We soon found one who was only too willing to take us in exchange for a half-dozen tins of food, as the local population were craving food as much as we were. For the next few days a dozen of us lived off the bounty of our trip to Singapore, and we climaxed the event with a birthday party for one of our mates till none of us could eat any more. The feeling was wonderful!

A few days later my application to join an official truck party to Singapore was granted, and I went in to Orchard Road to retrieve the valuable shorthand diary and papers which I had buried there.

Finding our old camp site was simple, but it was a much more difficult task to locate the exact spot where I had buried my diary eight months earlier, as all of the huts had been pulled down and the area was now quite bare.

After almost an hour of fruitless searching for the stepped-out spot ten paces from the now non-existent hut doorway, I was on the point of abandoning all hope of finding my precious diary and papers when I struck something solid and was excited to find my buried canister! The contents were in perfect condition, so after returning the spade borrowed from the Malay owner over the fence, we then sat down in his garage and shared fourteen small bottles of Tiger beer!

Back at Changi, messages were beginning to filter through from Australia by wireless through Radio Australia and for the first time I was given an opportunity to see one of the radio sets which had been operating, this one concealed in the wall of a basement cell in the gaol!

Being one of maybe a few writers of shorthand in the gaol, I was handed the dubious but exclusive distinction of taking down the long series of personal messages being transmitted from Australia each morning. Not having written shorthand at the speed of speech for so many years, I was naturally out of practice, so it was an unenviable task trying to transcribe my notes at Camp HQ afterwards.

Many of the messages did not, of course, reach the men for whom they were intended. Some had left Changi for Burma, Japan, Borneo, and so on, and many others were dead.

Red Cross supplies of food and medication began to make a startling difference to the health and appearance of the men. With the Red Cross supplies came representatives to ascertain how best to satisfy the immediate requirements of the camp. Naturally, European foodstuffs still had to be rationed, so for the time being we were compelled to maintain rice as the basis for lots of the cooking.

Lady Mountbatten was made fully aware of this fact when, on one of her very early visits to Changi gaol, she struck a team of our mess orderlies leaving the kitchen to serve mess in our company lines. 'My, but don't they look lovely!' said Lady Mountbatten, eyeing the tray of small doovers Junior Johnson was carrying. 'Yeah', retorted Junior smartly, 'but they're still bloody rice!'

The remark raised the ire of a nearby NCO, who wanted to slap Junior on a charge sheet. Junior did not know (nor I am sure would he have cared) who Lady Mountbatten was, and she was 'big' enough to have taken his remark in good part.

Since our arrival at the gaol in 1944, the only flag we had seen flown from the mast head at the entrance to the gaol had been the Japanese 'flaming circle'. However, all ranks were notified that the Union Jack would be raised by our British Camp Commander at a special ceremony next morning. Members of our unit took up a position on the flat roof of our unit building so that we could witness to the full this memorable occasion.

The incident could, and should, have represented the finale to our term as prisoners of the Japanese. However, the special flag-raising ceremony on the high tower above the gaol was hardly visible or in the hearing of those of our unit who had paraded to witness it.

As if to anti-climax the whole disappointing affair, our flag rose slowly to the top of the mast head and lay there limply without the slightest movement in the still air.

Instead of the enthusiastic cheering which all of us expected, the men remained silent, then simply broke off and returned to their quarters.

Upon liberation, a similar disappointment befell Harold Payne — latterly the well-known and popular president of the British FEPOW (Far Eastern Prisoner of War) Association — who found himself still in Thailand, several years after the railway had been completed. Harold had dreamed of those first few words of greeting from our liberators, but he was somewhat taken aback when a gun-toting Yank dropped out of the sky and declared: 'You bastards stink'. My good friend Harold Payne is still getting over the shock!

A few days after our flag-raising ceremony, word came through that the first party would soon be selected for return to Australia by plane. I do not know why, but our area of the camp was chosen from which to take the few lucky ones to make up the party. Naturally men suffering from dysentery, recurring malaria, etc. could not be considered for the trip, so by process of elimination a list was compiled of those fit enough to front the medical officer for final acceptance. Having been fit enough to qualify for every working party called for from our unit, I felt there was nothing much wrong with me now that would disqualify me for a simple plane trip. Nor was there.

Doc Wickham did the medical examination of our chaps, and we soon learned those who had been declared fit to travel. A couple of injections, an issue of boots, tropical uniforms, underwear, etc. and we were ready to depart early next morning.

• • •

We said goodbye to our mates as we climbed into the trucks, and watched the walls we had come to know so well fade into the distance as we moved off in the direction of the flying-boat base out on the Straits of Johore.

We were met at the entrance to the air force camp by a Red Cross worker, who handed out a packet of cigarettes to each man, and were then shown to the quarters we were to occupy. We expected to depart the same day, but learned that one of the Catalina flying boats had developed engine trouble and we would have to await its arrival from Labuan.

In the meantime, we were free to poke around the camp and the shores of the Johore Straits. A few of us discovered a huge flying boat moored near a small jetty, and were invited aboard by the English officer in charge. We were pleased to accept, and more pleased when we learned that we were to be permitted to remain aboard while the plane made a circuit of Singapore island.

Few of us had flown before, and certainly none of us in a Sunderland Flying Boat. It was a huge plane, with an upper and lower deck and plenty of room for all of us to move about, and although each of us knew Singapore island backwards from the ground level, it was something else to see it from the air.

The experience was thrilling, and gave us a foretaste of the joy that was to be ours when we were to eventually fly home to Australia. The flight took us over the Changi area and then down around Keppel Harbour and the docks, where dozens of our war ships were lying, looking for all the world to us like small toys.

Next morning we took off on the first leg of our long journey, but before leaving the island the planes flew us back to take our last glimpse of Changi. I made a small parachute from a spare khaki handkerchief and string, attached a packet of cigarettes and addressed the note to Tom Walters, our Unit RSM. At the appropriate time, the rear gunner opened the trap, and away went the small message down to Changi gaol. Tom did not receive the note or the cigarettes, but no doubt someone in Changi enjoyed a few Australian smokes!

There were 16 POWs on our plane, and as there were only about ten Catalinas we realised how fortunate we had been, as the journey by boat would have been so much slower.

It was not possible to see out of the plane from where most of us were squatted, so we soon arranged a roster for the best viewing sites. The rear gunner's seat was a particularly good spot, as was the one up with the pilot.

Most of the men in our aircraft were of the 4th MT, but we also had WO1 Doug Leathart, who became a Deputy Commissioner of Repatriation, and Bert Downer, a federal Member of Parliament in later years, so unbeknown to us we had in our party two men who were later to play important roles in Australia's post-war reconstruction. At the time, however, our praise was all for our crew—the angels who were so speedily returning us to Australia.

Our two pilots were FO Newman of Claremont, Western Australia, and Harry Scott of Toronto, New South Wales, plus five others including rear-gunner Sgt. Phil Dean, whose main job seemed to be to act as host to his lousy-looking lot of passengers.

We made Labuan Island toward late afternoon, and as we came down we could see that some of the other Cats had already arrived. A naval vessel pulled up alongside, and we scrambled aboard, with a word of thanks to the crew as we departed.

Having been out of the war—more or less—for so long, we knew nothing of landing craft, army ducks and the like, and naturally expected our transport to dump us off at the pier or thereabouts, but were amazed when it sailed right up the beach and then continued up to the roadway! The 'duck' took us to a hospital camp several miles down the road, where for the first time we met again sisters of the Australian Nursing Service—they looked beautiful in their white uniforms and veils.

That night, we sat down to a meal of roast lamb, potatoes, green peas, and delicious peaches—eaten with a knife, fork and spoon for the first time in three and a half years!

The next surprise in store was our accommodation for the night. There, lined along either side of our large tent were hospital beds, made up with beautiful white sheets and mosquito nets. It was really too much to take so suddenly, and we protested to the nurses that we were not used to mosquito nets and did not need them—the nurses won!

As if all this were not enough, the nurses added further to our cupful of happiness by bringing around bundles of letters from home. I think I finished up with five or six, including a three-page typed foolscap edition from one of my sisters. She had been given the task of writing to inform me that my fiancee had, during my absence, married some other bloke! However, the news was not altogether unexpected as there had been a complete absence of any mention of her in the short messages I had received for some time from other members of the family. We all went to sleep that night feeling very happy with our lot, enjoying to the full the feel of the clean white sheets and pillow-cases, and slept soundly till we were awakened by the sound of Reveille.

The QM at the hospital had certainly provided himself with an adequate supply of all equipment and clothing, so we spent most of the morning relieving him of some of it — new shorts, shirts, underwear, hats, eating utensils, and all the other additions to make us look and feel something like well-dressed soldiers.

We had all commenced to put on weight since the arrival of our own food at Changi a few weeks previously, and could feel and see the difference in ourselves as the bones began to disappear under healthy flesh. By the time I reached home I had put on over 12 kg, with my face puffed up like a football and trying to wear shorts that refused to meet in the middle!

In the afternoon we were invited to visit a nearby camp occupied by Australian sailors. In an old *attap* hut, the walls of which were decorated by scores of the sailors' favourite 'pin-up' girls in various stages of undress, we talked of our experiences over a few glasses of good old Aussie beer. We had been warned to be back at the hospital by 4 pm to prepare for departure, so left our sailor friends long before the tales had all been told.

We were issued with plenty of tinned rations, and climbed into the Catalinas just before dusk, everyone feeling highly excited at the thought that next time we set foot to ground it would be on Australian soil, as we were to fly through the night to Darwin. Few of us slept for long that night, as we were all too excited to think and talk of anything else but what it would be like to be back in Aussie again and the glorious welcome that awaited us from our families and friends.

The old Catalinas just plugged on through the night at a steady speed, in spite of a storm which pitched and tossed us around for a while — however, the battering our tummies had received as prisoners precluded any possibility of the boys succumbing to anything as insignificant as plane sickness!

The navigator warned us as we were approaching the Australian coast, and all of us jostled around the few small windows which would give us our first view of Australia's shores. In the half-light just before dawn, we strained our eyes to make out the dim outline of the coast, and as it gradually became visible we became more excited than a crowd of hysterical schoolgirls.

The Catalina glided down to a perfect landing and roared its own welcome as it skimmed across the water to a halt.

Within a few minutes we had disembarked and were making our way onto what we could now see was an isolated section of the beach, with a background of thick scrub into which a dusty old track disappeared.

We did not know whether we expected a party to greet us on landing, but none of us could help but feel that no matter who might have been there, they could not have been more Australian than the kangaroo which leisurely hopped across our path as we made our way up from the beach.

It was as if he had appeared to convince us that we were really back in our homeland, and was there as if to say: 'Welcome home Digger'.

Glossary

A.A.S.C.	Australian Army Service Corps
A.G.H.	Australian General Hospital
attap huts	huts on bamboo frames with roof covering of large dried palm leaves
back-up	usually an alphabetical system at mess parade to serve any remaining food
bamboo-rod	rod inserted into the anus to check for cholera or dysentery
benjo	word used to seek permission from a guard to visit the toilet
blachan	native fish paste with an extremely strong smell
boiki	sick
bore hole	latrine
buggeroo	word used by the Japanese to show annoyance when a POW did something which displeased them
bukit timahs	scrotal dermatitis
canary	secret radio
C.C.S.	Casualty Clearing Station
chunkel/chunkle	large hoe
cop the crow	unlucky, being given a distasteful job
doover	anything resembling a rissole
drongo	someone considered to be an idiot
dummy dummy	Japanese expression of displeasure
dung punch	medical inspection to check for dysentery or cholera
eggety-puffs	small local Chinese/Malay pastie with tasty ingredients
furphy	a rumour. The word originated during World War I when doubtful stories were brought back by soldiers after visiting the army 'Furphy' water tanks. A descendant, Charles Furphy from Corop in Victoria, was a member of our unit.
G-string	small piece of material threaded through the legs and then tied around the waist

get set	term used in the game of two-up
glass-rod	same as bamboo-rod or dung punch
happy feet	tingling sensation in the feet caused by vitamin deficiency
ichi bung	Japanese for number one, or anything good
kashira hidari	eyes left
kashira migi	eyes right
kempei tai	Japanese secret police
kurrah	Japanese order, often delivered fiercely
kybosh	prevent, put a stop to
lead-swinger	a bludger
monkey	long fan-shaped pulley used to raise and sink the wooden piles of the wooden railway bridges
motte-koi	a Japanese command to come here
NCO	Non Commissioned Officer
O.Rs.	Other Ranks
padang	Malay playing field
pap	soft, easily digestible dish made from ground rice
pellagra	vitamin deficiency disease often affecting the mouth
R.A.P.	Regimental Aid Post
scrounger	one with ability to forage for food or items useful to wellbeing
shoot through	to escape
speedo	expression used by the Japanese urging POWs to hurry and work harder
swi	slang word for the game of two-up
t'adapa	Malay expression for doesn't matter
tenko	roll call
tomtits	dysentery
towgay	long green shoots similar to bean shoots
tunkah	makeshift carrier made from an old rice sack for carrying rocks or soil
white jap	derogatory term to describe anyone too friendly with the Japanese
yak	beast of burden similar to a small bullock
yesame/*yasumi*	Japanese word for rest/smoko/ holiday

Index